BECOMING
NEHEMIAH

LEADING WITH SIGNIFICANCE

DAVID L. MCKENNA

Beacon Hill Press of Kansas City
Kansas City, Missouri

Copyright 2005
by Beacon Hill Press of Kansas City

ISBN 083-412-2170

Cover Design: Brandon Hill

Library of Congress Cataloging-in-Publication Data

McKenna, David L. (David Loren), 1929-
    Becoming Nehemiah : leading with significance / David L. McKenna.
        p. cm.
    ISBN 0-8341-2217-0 (pbk.)
    1. Christian leadership—Biblical teaching 2. Nehemiah (Governor of Judah)
3. Bible. O.T. Nehemiah—Criticism, interpretation, etc. I. Title.

    BS1365.6.L4M35 2005
    222'.806—dc22

                                                    2005025404

10 9 8 7 6 5 4 3 2 1

CONTENTS

INTRODUCTION

Why another book on the leadership of Nehemiah? What more can be said after so many good books on the subject have been published? The answer begins in the Word of God.

Job compares the human search for wisdom to a miner tunneling into the depths of the earth with the hope of finding the purest of gold and the most precious of gems. Wisdom, however, is the jewel that still eludes him. For human understanding at its best, wisdom is just a rumor that reaches the ears until God steps in. Then, like the master jeweler who appraises a gem, tests its clarity, and confirms its value, God reveals the secret of the ages: "The fear of the LORD—that is wisdom, and to shun evil is understanding" (Job 28:28). The Book of Nehemiah is like a deep mine with veins of truth yet to be explored. Leadership is only one of those veins, and it is not exhausted. We can count on the next generation of biblical miners sending deep probes into the truth and discovering priceless gems. God himself will continue to honor the search with fresh revelation given by the mind of His Spirit.

The Advancement of Theory

Another reason for writing a book on Nehemiah comes with the serious study of leadership. We may be fooled by the number of popular books on leadership that crowd the shelves of our bookstores. Most of them are thick on marketing and thin on theory. In between these best-sellers, however, are books based upon scholarly study, sound testing, and thoughtful writing. These are the books that are advancing the substance of the field so fast that leadership may well become a discipline deserving its own niche in academic libraries. Without pretending to be a front-runner in the field, I see myself applying some of these insights to the study of Nehemiah's leadership. Another analogy comes to mind. Karl Barth described American pioneers as men and women who made their way into the wilds with the Bible in one hand and a newspaper in the other. The implication is that the two sources of knowledge complement each other —the truth of the Bible shedding light on current events and the facts of the newspaper adding insights into biblical truth. By the same token, I see the Word of God shedding light on leadership development and leadership theory expanding our insights into biblical truth. Nehemiah's story is so replete with meaning for the study of leadership that it's a prime candidate for this joint venture into truth.

The Christian Quest

If you really want to know why I write, you must know my heart. As I watch the Christian community cast its lot for the future on the development of leadership, I fear that we will fall into another pit of promises that can't be fulfilled. Over the past five decades, I've watched Christianity hitch its wagon to any number of shooting stars—crusades, personal evangelism, church growth, church planting, conservative politics, opinion polls, marketing techniques, and now leadership development. While each of these thrusts has value, they fail when they're perceived as the panacea for the ills of the Church and the guarantee for the fulfillment of the Great Commission. Without a realistic approach to leadership development, it will go the way of its predecessors—full of promise but failing to produce. Forgive me one more biblical analogy. Jesus curses the fig tree for having leaves that promise fruit for His hunger but show barren branches underneath. Our obsession with leadership development is like that. It promises so much but produces so little. To capture a cliché, style without substance or, as the Texans say, "all hat, no cattle" may be our downfall. Unless leadership development produces the fruit that satisfies our urgent needs, it will go the way of our earlier promises.

But I have a problem. I still believe that leadership development is the key to the future of the faith. Jesus relies upon leadership development for His disciples in order to assure the spread of the gospel and the establishment of His Church. We dare not, then, let secular theory overwhelm biblical theology. If we do, we'll be left with the same taste of burnt ashes in our mouth that have come with our giddy expectations for winning the world by secular means. If only we can fashion the development of Christian leadership on biblical terms, we have a chance. It will not be easy, because so many of the promises of biblical leadership directly contradict the premises of secular leadership. Nehemiah, however, gives us a chance to find the balance between the two. Without compromising his biblical convictions, he serves with full integrity in the most difficult of secular settings. So my purpose in writing is to let Nehemiah teach us how a servant leads, whether we're clergy or laity, when the odds are against us and outcomes are in doubt. In Nehemiah we see repudiation of the idea that leadership is easy and that the outcomes are assured. Once we take him off the pedestal of celebrity status, we join him on a journey of leadership that matches the reality of our own pathway.

The Block-and-Gap Method

The more we delve into the leadership of Nehemiah, the

more he grows on us. Rather than assuming that our text is the final answer to his success, we acknowledge that we're only dipping into his experience. Therefore, we don't follow the pattern of commentaries that print sections of Scripture in bulk and then interpret them one by one. Instead, we've chosen what's called the "block-and-gap" method of teaching in order to emphasize salient points. Harvard University uses this method for courses that cover extended periods of time or include large masses of information, such as the history of Western civilization. The Book of Nehemiah qualifies for this method because of the breadth and the depth of its story. Even more selective decisions about "blocks" and "gaps" of textual material become necessary when Nehemiah's leadership is the focus of the study. To assist the reader, the "blocks" of Scripture chosen for this study precede the chapters that relate to each stage in Nehemiah's leadership development. By first letting the scripture speak for itself, the reader will be able to coordinate the biblical text with the book text. "Gaps" in the text will immediately become obvious and lead to the recommendation that the reader take the time to read and reread the whole text of the Book of Nehemiah from different versions of the Old Testament. With each reading, the Spirit of God will give new insights to correct, confirm, and enlarge the writing of this book.

Developing Our Leadership

Wherever we turn, whether in secular or religious fields, the development of leadership has become the hope for the renewal of society, its institutions, and the Church itself. At times it seems as if everyone is talking about leadership development, but no one is doing anything about it. Rather, we expect that potential leaders will be motivated to apply the principles of development on their own. This is certainly the case in most of the popular books on leadership. Insights are galore, but application is limited. As part of a corrective on this omission, the intention of this book is to invite every reader into a personal leadership journey hand in hand with Nehemiah. At the end of each chapter, the insights drawn from Nehemiah's experience are brought together as a practical exercise that we can apply to our own experience at any stage or in any position of leadership. The exercises are designed to be developmental. Beginning with the elemental task of working a plan, the challenge rises to the complexity of leading from paradox. The exercises are also designed to be interactive. Although an individual reader can grow in the understanding of leadership by applying the insights from Nehemiah's experience to his or her own journey, the value is multiplied if the reader partners with other readers who are on their own journey. Leadership development at its best will always include open communication, objective criticism, and obliging accountability among peers. A prayer, therefore, accompanies these exercises. May the Spirit of God be our Teacher, our Counselor, and our Guide as we learn to lead by being the first to serve.

With this prayer, I invite you to join me on Nehemiah's journey into greatness. Even though he lived and served almost 2,500 years ago, his story is as fresh as the latest book on leadership that stands at the top on the best-seller list.

PART 1
INTO THE FIRE

If anyone wants to be first, he must be the very last, and the servant of all (Mark 9:35).

—Jesus' definition of greatness

1
THE MAN AND HIS JOURNEY
A REAL-TIME LOOK AT NEHEMIAH

NEHEMIAH is extolled as an ideal leader among Old Testament people of character. He is best known for his work of rebuilding the walls of Jerusalem against all odds. The feat commends his character as a man of God and his competence as a leader of note. Also, as a practical leader who "gets things done," he has a special appeal to our success-oriented society. In this context, Nehemiah illustrates our tendency to make biblical characters larger than life when we want to make a point. Perhaps this is why Nehemiah is a favorite subject of contemporary books on Christian leadership. After all, anyone who can rebuild the walls of a city in 52 days gets celebrity status in the Christian community. Nehemiah deserves better. If we reverse the engines and introduce a note of reality into the story of his leadership, we discover an ordinary man on a perilous journey with whom we can identify.

A Realistic Look at the Situation

If the opportunity for leadership is defined in the contemporary terms of location, position, and authority, Nehemiah is severely handicapped. As a *Jew* exiled in a pagan land and held down under the boot of a despotic king, he has little chance to rise as a leader of his people. More than that, as one of the ambitious Jews who accommodates themselves to the Babylonian culture in order to survive, Nehemiah has to arouse suspicion among his peers. While his role as the king's cupbearer attests to his integrity and his loyalty, he is first and foremost a *servant*. In the ancient East, the position of cupbearer is commonly conceived as a butler serving the whims and fancies of a dictator. His greatest handicap, however, is his status as a member of the *laity*. Historically, leadership for Israel is in the hands of patriarchs, priests, judges, and prophets who are visited by God and anointed by His Spirit.

Instead, Nehemiah comes home to Israel with the authority granted by a secular king because of the "gracious hand of God." This explains why his first foray around the walls to survey the situation comes under cover of darkness. Like a prophet without honor in his own country, we can understand how he might be received as a carpetbagger coming from exile without the status of position or the authority of God. Finally, Nehemiah has the challenge to serve a *secular* role in a religious setting. His leadership task of rebuilding the walls requires the skill of an engineer, and his responsibility for rebuilding or reforming the nation calls for the competence of a governor. Although he is in full support of the moral and spiritual foundations for these tasks, he leaves the sacred functions to Ezra, the high priest, and his compatriots among the Levites.

With these apparent handicaps, Nehemiah deserves our highest respect as a layperson who takes the risk of a secular role in order to influence moral and spiritual change. This is the acid test of Godly leadership. It is one thing to come to leadership in a religious setting with the credentials of sacred ordination, and quite another to find ministry in a secular role without any sacred authority other than one's own devotion and a servant spirit.

A Realistic Look at God

Sooner or later, each of us will find ourselves in a leadership challenge similar to Nehemiah's. In the mid-1970s Daniel J. Evans, governor of the state of Washington in the United States, asked me to chair his select committee to study gambling after the people passed a referendum that reversed a long-time prohibition against games of chance. Because the referendum permitted everything from bingo to casino games and lotteries, the governor wanted me to help prepare legislation that drew lines on the limits. All my preaching and teaching about our Christian responsibility for the moral climate of our culture came back to haunt me. After prayer and counsel, I accepted the appointment and found myself in a "no-man's land" of secular politics.

As Nehemiah was called into leadership as a Jewish layperson who held the position as a butler in the court of a pagan king, I was a member of the clergy from the Christian community who believed in the evils of gambling. The media had a heyday with my appointment, and civic leaders cautioned me about the threat of violence. Nevertheless, we moved ahead, giving fairness to all voices, researching the facts in other states, and finally making a recommendation that permitted bingo, raffles, and pull tabs but prohibited casino games and a state-run lottery.

Through that experience, I know why Nehemiah had such confidence in the sovereignty of God. Every day that I presided over sessions of the commission, I began that day by throwing myself on the mercy of God. Never before or never since have I been so dependent upon Him. Like Nehemiah, I prayed for Him to support me in the initial decision, strengthen me in times of conflict, save me from my

s, and remember me with favor when I wrote a mi-
...ority report opposing the final recommendation of the
commission. Out of that experience, I call for a realistic look
at Nehemiah, the man and the leader.

A Realistic Look at the Man

Early on, we learn that Nehemiah is a *loyal* man. Long
before he has been entrusted to be the cupbearer to the
king, he has to pass the most strenuous test of loyalty. He is
an Israelite in exile, and natural mistrust will follow him.
King Artaxerxes has every reason to suspect that a Jew
might try to poison him to start a coup or seek vengeance
for an exiled nation. Whatever the testing process, Nehemiah wins the complete confidence of the king as a loyalist
whom he can trust implicitly. At the same time, there is no
hint in Scripture that Nehemiah compromises his faith even
though statues of Artaxerxes stand on virtually every corner
in Babylon. Subjects of the king have to worship at these
shrines under the threat of death, but somehow Nehemiah
wins an exemption as a Jew who refuses to bow at a graven
image. We are reminded of King Herod calling John the
Baptist for private conferences and King Festus coming so
close to belief after meeting Paul the apostle. Even despots
have a nose for the genuine.

With the courage of his convictions, Nehemiah shows us
what it means to be a *confident* man. Throughout his autobiography, we meet a man who knows how to live under authority. He respects and obeys the dictatorial rule of King
Artaxerxes but holds the sovereignty of God as his supreme
authority. When he says, "The gracious hand of my God was
upon me" (2:8), "The God of heaven will give us success"
(2:20), or "what God had put in my heart" (2:12), we are in-

troduced to a man who has such confidence in the sovereignty of God that he is willing to take risks in His name. What a delicate balance! With just the slightest push to one side or the other, Nehemiah can become a crusading tyrant or a cowering milquetoast. But instead, he rides on the razor's edge to show the power and glory of his God. Confidence in the sovereign Lord is an indispensable quality of godly leadership in any generation.

Total obedience to the will of God does not rob Nehemiah of his freedom. As witnessed by the spirit of his prayers, he is a *devout* man who has an intimate relationship with his Lord. He can confess his part in the sins of his people, ask for assurance in his plans, plead for strength while working, call for intervention when attacked, join the people in thanksgiving, and express doubts about the success of his leadership. None of these prayers is an official petition required by the Law or in the liturgy of worship. They spring from the heart of a believer who has the spiritual capital to test his faith in a secular arena, such as the court of King Artaxerxes, or in a secular role, such as the provincial governor of Jerusalem and Judah.

Will the real Nehemiah stand up? When he does, we see a person who comes to leadership with a balance of situational handicaps and personal assets. Because he is so much like us, we can learn more from his experience than if he is touted as an idealistic hero of an ancient time with a storybook life. The same touch of realism is needed as we contemplate joining him on his leadership journey.

A Realistic Look at His Journey

As noted earlier, Nehemiah's leadership is the subject of many good books in Christian literature. How do we account for his popularity? We have also noted that Nehemiah appeals to our contemporary interest in leadership because he is a doer who gets results. In our rush to learn from him, however, there is a tendency to make his journey into leadership look like a straight line moving upward from one success to another. Like so many cut-and-print models of leadership, then, realism discourages us when we try to take the model home. This error is not fatal. By introducing realism into our introduction of Nehemiah's journey, we not only temper the idealism that causes the model to fail but also create a climate of understanding that keeps us from discouragement.

A realistic look at Nehemiah's journey begins with the fact that his leadership is *developmental* rather than static. Or in common language, leadership is a journey, not a jaunt. Many of the books written on Nehemiah's experience follow the format of a biblical commentary in which portions of Scripture are interpreted as if they were stand-alone segments. This approach creates the impression that leadership is a series of discrete events without developmental continuity. In each of these events, the commentator finds some leadership principles that can be applied in the contemporary scene. The result, however, is the framing of a picture of leadership as a montage of events and responses. We know that this is not the case. Leadership is an ongoing process of development with all the starts, stops, and spurts of a pilgrimage. Snapshots will not do. We need a nonstop video camera to record the action and the progress. Once we start the camera rolling, Nehemiah's leadership journey becomes a dynamic movement with which we can personally identify.

Another note of realism reminds us that Nehemiah's leadership experience is *situational* rather than individual. More often than not, individuals are thrust into leadership situations rather than seeking them out. Still, the debate goes on. Is effective leadership weighted toward individual traits or situational circumstances? Or is it a balance of these factors? The answers to these questions will determine whether or not we can teach leadership in a classroom and then put the learning to test in the "real" world. Books on Nehemiah's leadership put the weight upon the character and competence of the man. His situation in the different settings of Babylon, Jerusalem, and Israel is not ignored, but the influence of these settings upon his leadership style and his effectiveness is not given the emphasis it deserves. Once we insert these diverse settings into the developmental process, Nehemiah's leadership takes on a different cast from which we can learn to adapt, change, and grow. Once we add the richness of the changing background into the moving picture of Nehemiah's journey, our study takes on the reality of learning to lead in a time when the speed of change is compared to a ball field with a moveable left field fence. Yesterday's home runs become today's easy outs.

Realism enters the scene again when we realize that leadership development is *complex* rather than simplistic. A cut-and-print approach to leadership appeals to a popular market that is eager for a "quick fix" in executive action. One-minute solutions, easily remembered analogies, and lists of "how to" phrases may sell books and fill up seminars, but they fall short for leadership when the chips are down. Leadership is complex, messy, and filled with contradiction. Paradox, ambiguity, and surprise are the stuff of which leadership is made. If Nehemiah were to come alive and read some of the books that have simplified and sanitized his leadership today, he would probably scream, "You don't have a ghost of an idea what I went through!" In fairness to him, we need to delve into the complexity that makes his leadership so much like our experience today. More than seeing Nehemiah stride triumphantly over circumstances in the ever-changing scene, we need to walk in his sandals as he struggles with complexities and contingencies in his uneven pilgrimage.

At the risk of criticism, a realistic look at Nehemiah's leadership journey exposes the tendency to spiritualize the experience at the expense of his *humanity*. There is no doubt whatsoever about the spiritual integrity and maturity of Nehemiah. We have already seen that he is a loyal, confident, and devout man of God. His spiritual depth is a constant that commends him as a model for godly leadership and carries him through success and failure. A problem arises, however, if the glow of his character blurs a realistic look at his competence. In a very practical way, Nehemiah shows us skills of planning, organizing, and implementing to achieve results. He never uses his spirituality as a substitute for those skills. In the book that bears his name, we encounter all the passions of conflict, frustration, success, and failure that make up the human experience of leadership. In these passions, we see Nehemiah as one of us. By seeing how his spirituality and his humanity work together under the call of God, we join Nehemiah on the pilgrimage of leadership. With him, we find that the constancy of our devotion is a holding power for the contingencies of change.

Nehemiah deserves to be honored as a leader par excellence, but on a journey into leadership that is developmental, situational, complex, and human. He is a work in progress whose leadership is tested in a variety of situations that challenge him anew and reveal both his strengths and his weaknesses. A realistic reading of Nehemiah's story does not diminish the nature of revelation or downplay the spiritual lessons to be learned. Quite the opposite. One of proofs for the divine inspiration of Scripture is the unvarnished truth about all of our biblical heroes, whether prophet, priest, and king in the Old Testament, or apostle, deacon, and disciple in the New Testament. Nehemiah joins this company as a flesh-and-blood leader under the call of God with whom we can identify and from whom we have much to learn.

Developing Our Leadership
Exercise 1

How would you write an autobiography of your leadership journey to this point in time? Begin by choosing a title for the book that sums up your experience. Name each stage of your journey as a chapter, and combine the chapters into a table of contents. Be creative. Let the names of the chapters realistically describe a pilgrimage that has its starts and stops, detours and dilemmas, intersections and turning points. As an example, I traced my own journey under the title *Astounding Grace*, because I came to leadership against overwhelming odds. Perhaps you can feel the ebb and flow of my lifetime journey in the titles of these chapters:

1. A Brand from the Burning
2. The Kid from Across the Tracks
3. The Pain of Growing Up Holy
4. Awakened by Greatness
5. An Academic Crabwalk
6. A Sanctifying Moment
7. You Can Go Home Again
8. The Road Not Taken
9. A Quantum Leap
10. Fifteen Minutes of Fame

Put your story to the same test. Is it intriguing? Does it reflect reality? Will it teach others? Do the end results honor your character and competence and glorify God? Our story tells that we are human, we are fallible, we are blessed, and we are chosen. Some of us become leaders, and others falter along the way. What makes the difference? The answer may be in an experience called the "crucible," where character is tested and competence is learned.

*When he has
tested me, I will
come forth
as gold*
(Job 23:10).

—Job's faith in the
crucible of suffering

2
THE CRUCIBLE
A TEST OF CHARACTER AND COMPETENCE

ARE LEADERS born or made? This unanswered question takes its place in the same forum that asks whether human personality is determined by nature or nurture. To date, no geneticist has isolated a gene that identifies born leaders, and psychologists still struggle in their search for a trait that sorts our leaders from nonleaders. On the other side, sociologists and historians cannot agree on the circumstances or events that bring a person into leadership. To try to answer whether leaders are born or made is to work with the underside of a crazy quilt in which we see the knots but have to guess the pattern.

Leadership development is equally knotty and complex. How do we identify future leaders? What do they need to know about theories of leadership? What kind of experiences should be part of their preparation? How can we predict their success or failure? Where do we begin?

The Model of the Crucible

Warren Bennis and Robert Thomas have written an intriguing book titled *Geeks and Geezers* (Boston: Harvard Business School Press, 2002). Using a survey of corporate leaders as the basis for their study, the authors propose a model of leadership development that includes four factors:

1. The *context* is the era in which leaders are developed.

2. The *character* is the values that individuals bring to leadership.

3. The *crucible* of experience is the place of testing where leaders are prepared.

4. The *competencies* for leadership are the proficiencies for future leadership that are shaped in the crucible (89).

A synopsis of Bennis and Thomas's writing on each of these factors will show how their model for leadership development works.

The Context. Geezers are senior leaders born in 1925 or after whose lives have been shaped by the Great Depression and World War II. They are the products of the Era of Limits. Geeks are young leaders under the age of 30 who were born after 1975 and into a time of affluence, high technology, and a global economy. They are products of the Era of Options. The personal values that these two generations bring to leadership are worlds apart.

The Character. Geezers have the goal of making a living, while geeks want to make a life. Geezers learn from history, while geeks want to make history. Geezers are geared to external success, while geeks are more interested in internal self-identity. Geezers seek stability, while geeks seek significance. Geezers have a command and control style of leadership, while geeks tend to be more collaborative and creative. Geezers need a road map in order to lead, while geeks ask only for a compass. Geezers think of themselves as executives, while geeks prefer to be known as entrepreneurs. Geezers read the classics, while geeks surf the Net. Geezers have heroes, while geeks idolize celebrities.

On and on we could go, drawing the comparison between these two generations of leaders. In fact, we could stop right here and spend the rest of the time asking how we develop geeks who are leaders of the future. Or we could ask about the current generation of leaders who are someplace between geeks and geezers. Again, we could wonder about the effect of terrorism upon the next generation of leaders. Does 9/11 throw us back into an Era of Limits, not of material wealth but human freedom?

Our subject has more questions than it has answers. One thing we do know is that we cannot put a cut-and-print pattern of leadership development upon the future of the Church. As a geezer, I rely upon a mission statement and a strategic plan with key indicators for assessing results. But will the geeks of today and leaders of tomorrow ask only for a compass? If so, what is the compass that will give them a sense of direction? Our agenda for leadership in the future will have to include these questions.

The Crucible. Despite the wide range of differences between individual values that geeks and geezers bring to the table of leadership, Bennis and Thomas contend that they all have one thing in common. In preparation for leadership, they go through what the authors call the white heat of a "crucible" experience, in which their values are tested, often by adversity, and their competencies are honed, often at the risk of failure, for a future leadership role. The life stories of Nelson Mandela and John McCain are dramatic examples. In both cases, the suffering of imprisonment and torture does not break or destroy them. Instead, they come out of the crucible of suffering with the steely strength of self-identity and the farsighted vision for change that thrust them into leadership.

After reviewing the results of their model, Bennis and Thomas conclude that the crucible experience is so essential to the development of leaders that they are writing their next book under the title *The Crucible*. They feel as if they may have discovered a universal starting point for understanding how leaders are made, if not born.

The Competencies. According to Bennis and Thomas, the crucible is the place where the proficiencies for future leadership are fired, shaped, and honed: (1) the ability to adapt to changing circumstances, (2) a new view of the world in which they live, (3) a story that has meaning for others, and (4) an unblemished sense of personal integrity (121-22). One can readily see that these proficiencies are more than a skill set or tool kit for leadership. Flexibility, vision, meaning, and integrity are like the oils on an artist's palette. When applied to a canvas with deft brushstrokes of form, line, and color, leadership becomes an art.

Insights from the Crucible

The crucible is more than a classroom in which we learn about leadership. It is a laboratory in which we test our learning under the white heat of risk and, often, adversity. Out of this experience, *future leaders are discovered*. Bennis and Thomas write, "The ability to find meaning and strength in adversity distinguishes leaders from non-leaders" (108). To personalize this lesson, stop and think about great leaders of history or those who have founded our institutions and changed our lives. After reading or hearing their stories, I can remember crucible experiences for each of them. Our biblical heroes are known by the crucibles they experienced—Moses in the desert, David in the fields, Jesus in the wilderness, Peter in the courtyard, and Paul in Damascus. Even more personally, I expect that each of us who is called to lead can look back upon a crucible experience in our own lives.

Condoleezza Rice, Secretary of State for the United States, has served as one of the most powerful women in the world. As National Security Advisor to President George Bush, a position she served in prior to her current position, she made recommendations and decisions that will resound throughout the world for years to come. Yet without pretense, Rice speaks her Christian faith and confesses her dependence upon prayer. On the way to the top, she served as provost at Stanford University. With the responsibility for massive budget cuts and tough personnel decisions, she alienated faculty and students alike. While in the heat of this crucible, she preached a sermon at Menlo Park Presbyterian Church on the subject "The Privilege of Struggle" (*Christianity Today*, August 22, 2003). She said,

Struggle and sorrow are not license to give way to self-doubt, to self-pity, and to defeat, but an opportunity to find a renewed spirit and renewed strength to carry on. How else, but through struggle, are we to get to know the full measure of the Lord's capacity for intervention in our lives? If there are no burdens, how can we know that He can be there to lift them?

I suspect that Condoleezza Rice would identify her struggle in the position of provost at Stanford as the crucible experience that prepared her for one of the most demanding leadership roles in the world.

Rice leads us to another insight: *Even when future leaders fail while going through the crucible, they use it as an opportunity to learn, change, and grow.* The fact comes back to us time and time again. We learn, change, and grow more in adversity than in prosperity. The leadership journey travels along a corduroy road. Success is mixed with failure. It is failure, not success, that sorts out leaders from nonleaders. Invariably, when a leader fails, it is a learning experience for the person. When a nonleader fails, the whole world falls apart for him or her. My favorite story comes from another of Warren Bennis's books. Tom Watson, IBM's founder, called into his office a young executive who had just lost $10 million on a risk venture. Fearing the worst, the young executive said, "I expect that you want my resignation." Watson answered, "You can't be serious. We just spent 10 million dollars educating you!" (*Leaders: Four Strategies for Taking Charge* [New York: Harper and Row, 1985], 76). Watson's response typifies the attitude of future leaders in the crucible. Success is a catalyst, and failure is a teacher.

Our insights deepen as we realize that *the journey of leadership is the story of moving from one crucible to another as the individual moves higher in visibility and greater in responsibility.* Going back to the premise that preparation for leadership development is a journey rather than a jaunt, we see leaders advance from crucible to crucible as they move position to position. We also see that the heat is turned up in the crucible as the leader advances. Jesus, for instance, faces hypothetical questions from Satan in the crucible of the wilderness temptation. But when He comes to the Garden of Gethesmane, the issues escalate to life-and-death decisions of immediate consequence.

Jesus' real-time experience adds the most profound insight of all. *When we enter the crucible, we embark on two journeys— a leadership journey in which we rise in visibility and responsibility and a spiritual journey in which we descend to the depths of our character and faith.* Parker J. Palmer in his book *Let My Life Speak* (San Francisco: Jossey-Bass Publishers, 2000) writes that the spiritual journey is not like "a trouble-free 'travel package' sold by the tourism industry. It is more akin to the ancient pilgrimage—'a transformative journey to a sacred center' full of hardship, darkness and peril" (18). Later in the book, Parker refers to two thoughts about the spiritual journey, attributed to Annie Dillard. One is that the journey "will take us inward and downward, toward the hardest realities of our lives, rather than outward and upward toward abstraction, idealization, and exhortation. The spiritual journey runs counter to the power of positive thinking" (80). But then, as Dillard says, "If we ride those monsters all of the way down, we break through to something precious," a community of other travelers who have come to a place of "hidden wholeness" (80-81). While the leadership journey is characterized by "upward mobility" into visibility and responsibility, our spiritual journey is what Henri Nouwen calls "downward mobility" into the risk and adversity of self-giving love. The two paths cannot be walked separately. If they are, leadership leads to corruption, and spirituality leads to ineffectiveness. Taken together, however, they turn the paradox of "Christian leadership" into a cohesive force of character and competence that is unmatched in its influence for good.

The Servant Spirit

What has this to do with Nehemiah? Our hero is a prime example of a servant who comes out of the crucible of experience shaped by fire for the role of leadership. Nehemiah has the character to do the right things and the competence to get the right things done. As he rises in stature, he goes down deep in spirit. Success and failure go hand in hand with his popularity and adversity, celebration and despair. Leadership has its glamour, but not without its grit.

Join me, then, on Nehemiah's journey as he is shaped for leadership in the heat and pressure of the crucible as cupbearer to the king. Out of the fires of that experience, Nehemiah responds to the desperation of his people and becomes the engineer of God to rebuild the walls of Jerusalem in record time. Perhaps in recognition of his success, King Artaxerxes appoints him as governor of the province with an agenda to rebuild the nation and renew its spirit. Again, Nehemiah has unusual success as he joins with Ezra to restore God's covenant with His chosen people and reestablish the Law of Moses as the governing principle. But, sad to say, the purity of the nation is short-lived. When Nehemiah returns from Babylon for his second term in office, he finds the nation wallowing in moral and spiritual corruption. As despairing as it must have been, Nehemiah stays his course and becomes an aggressive reformer against unfaithful leaders who contaminate the holy Temple and violate their covenant with the holy God. Breathing a heavy sigh in his final prayer, he closes his book and disappears from the scene of biblical and secular history.

Unsung leaders of the laity will especially applaud Nehemiah as their hero. He is an ordinary man in secular exile who keeps his faith, loves his people, and does his duty. God does not call him or anoint him for his task. He simply responds to the needs of his people and finds that God's gracious hand is upon him. The drama of a burning bush may be lacking, and the stardom of a patriarch may be missing, but Nehemiah is one of us. Who knows what is ahead when God puts us in the crucible?

Developing Our Leadership
Exercise 2

How does the model of the crucible apply to our development as Christian leaders? We now see spiritual dimensions in Bennis and Thomas's model:

- *Context* is the age in which we are called to serve.
- *Character* is the spiritual integrity we bring to leadership.
- *The Crucible* is the place where we are tested by fire.
- *Competencies* are qualities shaped by fire for future leadership.

Let me give a personal example.

In my late 20s I was offered the position as an assistant professor of higher education at The Ohio State University. Although Christian higher education was still my calling, I felt as if I needed to prove my ability to do scholarly research and doctoral level teaching in a secular setting. Now I realize that I created my own crucible for learning how to lead. In my opening interview for the job, the heat in the crucible was turned up high. Ohio State was known as the hot bed for the instrumentalism of John Dewey and the behaviorism of B. F. Skinner, particularly in the School of Psychology and Education. When I appeared before the full faculty of the school prior to my appointment, the conversation opened with a cynical question, "What is a theist like you doing in a place like this?" Before I could answer, another professor challenged his colleague, "Why not? Are we afraid that he'll contaminate us?" From then, as I taught the history, philosophy, and curriculum of American higher education, I sharpened my understanding of Christian higher education in daily conversations with professors who openly professed their atheism or agnosticism in the classroom. When God called me back to the presidency of Spring Arbor College, I was ready to respond with a quickened mind and passionate heart. I had discovered the distinctive of Christian higher education in the concept of integrating faith, learning, and

living in the curriculum, on the campus, and after gradua-
tion. I saw that concept enacted in each institution where I
served. My life's motive, mission, and ministry were shaped
in the white heat of the crucible at Ohio State.

Now it is your turn. Out of the log that traces your journey into leadership (Exercise 1), ask yourself three questions: "What is the crucible that has had the most influence
upon my leadership today?" "How was my character tested?"
and "What competencies did I learn in the crucible that are
most evident in my leadership today?" You will be surprised
at the insights you gain from this exercise, especially when
you tell your story to a colleague and listen to his or her story as well.

PART 2
ON THE JOURNEY

I was cupbearer to the king (1:11).

—Nehemiah's preparation for leadership

Nehemiah's Leadership Journal
Chapters 1:1—2:10

Nehemiah's Call
(1:1-3)

In the month of Kislev in the twentieth year, while I was in the citadel of Susa, Hanani, one of my brothers, came from Judah with some other men, and I questioned them about the Jewish remnant that survived the exile, and also about Jerusalem.

They said to me, "Those who survived the exile and are back in the province are in great trouble and disgrace. The wall of Jerusalem is broken down, and its gates have been burned with fire."

Nehemiah's Confession
(1:4-11)

*When I heard these things, I sat down and wept. For some days I mourned and fasted and prayed before the God of heaven. Then I said: "O L*ORD*, God of heaven, the great and awesome God, who keeps his covenant of love with those who love him and obey his commands, let your ear be attentive and your eyes open to hear the prayer your servant is praying before you day and night for your servants, the people of Israel. I confess the sins we Israelites, including myself and my father's house, have committed against you. We have acted very wickedly toward you. We have not obeyed the commands, decrees and laws you gave your servant Moses. . . . saying, 'If you are unfaithful, I will scatter you among the nations, but if you return to me and obey my commands, then even if your exiled people are at the farthest horizon, I will gather them from there and bring them to the place I have chosen as a dwelling for my Name.' They are your servants and your people, whom you redeemed by your great strength and your mighty hand. O Lord, let your ear be attentive to the prayer of this your servant and to the prayer of your servants who delight in revering your name. Give your servant success today by granting him favor in the presence of this man." I was cupbearer to the king.*

Nehemiah's Commission
(2:1-6)

*In the month of Nisan in the twentieth year of King Arta-
xerxes, when wine was brought for him, I took the wine and gave
it to the king. I had not been sad in his presence before; so the
king asked me, "Why does your face look so sad when you are
not ill? This can be nothing but sadness of heart."*

*I was very much afraid, but I said to the king, "May the king
live forever! Why should my face not look sad when the city
where my fathers are buried lies in ruins, and its gates have been
destroyed by fire?"*

The king said to me, "What is it you want?"

*Then I prayed to the God of heaven, and I answered the king,
"If it pleases the king and if your servant has found favor in his
sight, let him send me to the city in Judah where my fathers are
buried so that I can rebuild it."*

*Then the king, with the queen sitting beside him, asked me,
"How long will your journey take, and when will you get back?"*

It pleased the king to send me; so I set a time.

Nehemiah's Courage
(2:7-10)

*I also said to him, "If it pleases the king, may I have letters to
the governors of Trans-Euphrates, so that they will provide me
safe-conduct until I arrive in Judah? And may I have a letter to
Asaph, keeper of the king's forest, so he will give me timber to
make beams for the gates of the citadel by the temple and for the
city wall and for the residence I will occupy?" And because the
gracious hand of God was upon me, the king granted my requests. So I went to the governors of Trans-Euphrates and gave
them the king's letters. The king had also sent army officers and
cavalry with me.*

*When Sanballat the Horonite and Tobiah the Ammonite official
heard about this, they were very much disturbed that someone
had come to promote the welfare of the Israelites.*

3
THE CUPBEARER
LEADERSHIP FOR SURVIVAL

EACH TIME I read Nehemiah's story, I am stopped by his statement "I was cupbearer to the king." This simple sentence is filled with meaning for understanding the leadership of Nehemiah. As cupbearer for the king, he is being prepared by God for the special task of rebuilding the walls of the Holy City. The model of the crucible helps us understand him and his preparation for leadership.

The Crucible of the Cupbearer

The Context of Exile. The story of Nehemiah's leadership journey begins with his serving as the cupbearer for the king of Babylon. Jews have been exiled in that distant land for 125 years. They are subjects of King Artaxerxes I (464-423 B.C.), the most dominant and dictatorial ruler among the kingdoms of the Middle East. Fifty years earlier, Ezra the priest and 50,000 Jews were given permission to return to Jerusalem in order to rebuild the city, the holy Temple, and its walls. They succeeded in building the Temple, but their attempt to rebuild the walls collapsed under assault from neighboring enemies. So as Nehemiah's story begins, the Jews in Jerusalem are a despised remnant, living among ruins, fearing for their safety, and languishing under the reproach of being "a worm" among nations. Back in Babylon, the Jews who did not return home in the original company are enjoying unusual success, especially in commercial ventures.

The Character of the Man. Nehemiah is a man who is

among the best and the brightest of the Jewish minority in exile. As cupbearer to a despotic king, he has taken the menial task of being a butler to the king and elevated it to the highest position of trust. Some students of ancient history even suggest that he might have become the confidant of the king with an informal influence equal to a prime minister. Despite his success and the temptations of the royal palace, he does not compromise his faith, forget his roots as a Jew, or abandon his life of devotion in prayer and worship.

The Fire of the Crucible. As cupbearer for the king, Nehemiah is in the white-hot heat of a crucible. Every day he lives with the ultimate risk of failure. He has only one task, and that is to assure the king's safety by taking the first sip of his wine. Every cue is read as he performs his task. A false smile or an unintended frown puts all systems on red alert. Like Nero in the Coliseum, just a turn of the king's thumb can mean death to the cupbearer. Sipping the wine is the defining moment, but preparing the wine is the leadership task.

Competencies Learned in the Crucible. What are the competencies that Nehemiah learns from the pressure cooker of the crucible? First and foremost, *Nehemiah learns to serve under authority.* It is an axiom of leadership that you cannot lead with authority until you learn to follow authority. In the case of Nehemiah, he is under the heel of an authoritarian boot. He has his choice. Will he be a wimp, a rebel, or a leader? The way in which an individual handles authority is a key to leadership development.

I recall two subordinates in institutions where I served. The first was a graduate of a military academy who had learned the meaning of orders and obedience. Even though our styles of leadership differed measurably, I knew I could always trust him to take charge in my absence without trying to usurp my authority or break the chain of command. Another member of one of my leadership teams proved to be the opposite. He had been abused by the inconsistent authority of an alcoholic father, and his brilliance thus carried the shadow of rebellious ambition. Time and time again, I had to deal with his attempts to undermine my authority, alienate his peers, and demean his subordinates. Our relationship vacillated between deference and defiance until the line of trust was broken and we had to part company. Whether for good or bad, the fire of the crucible determines how we handle authority.

As cupbearer for the king, *Nehemiah also learns how to analyze a situation and prepare a working plan.* His responsibility as cupbearer begins long before he takes a sip of wine from the king's cup. He has to have an overall plan and fail-safe process that reaches all of the way back to the vineyards where the grapes are grown and advances with exacting steps until the life-and-death moment when the cup is put to his lips.

One of the defining characteristics of effective leaders is the gift of being "first-class noticers." They see things that others do not. Long ago I read the biography of Bob Cousy, probably one of the greatest point guards in basketball history. Cousy's uncanny ability to make blind passes was explained by the fact that he had unusual peripheral vision so that he could see the whole floor at one time. Bennis and Thomas find this same gift among great leaders. They have a broader vision of the field for leadership action and see a wider range of options for leadership choices than nonleaders. In the simple sentence "I was cupbearer to the king," we can infer that Nehemiah is a first-class "noticer," seeing the scope of his task, making his plan, and understanding his options.

With his own life on the line, *Nehemiah is a quick learner who knows how to articulate a plan, command people, and pay attention to details.* When our life is at stake and survival is our motivation, there is no room for debate, delays, or indecision. Nehemiah has to act with precision, exercise authority over people, and avoid the slipups that can be fatal. It is often said, "God is in the details." For Nehemiah, his life is in the details. There seems little doubt that he is a perfectionist in dealing with every step in the process that brings wine to the king's table. One can imagine his developing a demanding process with personal checkpoints along the way. Just as the king's trust stops short of taking his word that the wine was safe to drink, Nehemiah has to take the same precaution with the vinters of royal vineyards and the sommeliers of royal wine cellars. He never enjoys the luxury of calling together focus groups before making a decision. More often than not, the result is "inclusion without conclusion." In this instance, Nehemiah has to be a hands-on leader with micromanagement as part of his style.

When dealing with a life-and-death decision at every meal, *Nehemiah learns how to anticipate conspiracy and adapt to crisis.* Artaxerxes' position as the most powerful of Middle Eastern kings makes him the prime target for external attacks and internal conspiracies. Because he cannot be voted out of office, he would have to be toppled from his throne by war, assassinated by guerillas, or betrayed by his own people. We can imagine the thick tension surrounding the preparation of every meal and every decanter of wine. Add then the rumors that will circulate and the real threats that will come—Nehemiah has to be a crisis manager with a nose for cues that might signal a conspiracy. When others panic, he has to remain consistent, steady, and faithful.

Finally, in the crucible of the cupbearer, *Nehemiah learns how to be accountable for the results of his work*. Usually when we talk about accountability, we are talking about qualitative, long-term, and often intangible results. Nehemiah's task does not permit him that privilege. Every time he puts a cup of wine to his lips, he lives or dies with the results of his work. Feedback is instantaneous. Educational theory tells us that students who get quick feedback on the quality of their work learn more and better than those whose feedback is delayed. If so, Nehemiah has to be a first-rate learner with daily reinforcement of the consequences.

Leadership for Survival

When a leader faces life-and-death decisions on a daily basis and survival is the all-consuming motive, it is no surprise to learn that Nehemiah's leadership style is both authoritarian and authoritative. He is authoritarian because his task gives him no margin for error; he is authoritative because his impeccable character earns the trust of his subordinates. Because his leadership is so narrowly defined, it limits the transfer of his style and systems to other situations. When life is at risk and survival is at stake, we need a nononsense leader whose word is law. Also, when we are dealing with a process that is narrowly defined, and the end product is a tangible target, we see that the competencies that Nehemiah learned in the crucible of the cupbearer are essential to success. Underlying the competencies, however, is the character of the man. Integrity, authenticity, and consistency are qualities that transfer with leadership in any situation.

Competencies from the Crucible

A summary of the competencies that Nehemiah learns in

the crucible as cupbearer to the king shows us how God readies him for the next level of leadership. Nehemiah learns to do the following:

1. Serve under authority
2. Analyze the situation
3. Activate the people
4. Attend to detail
5. Anticipate conspiracy
6. Adapt to crisis
7. Account for the results

Out of the heat of the crucible, Nehemiah is prepared for the challenge of leadership by learning competencies for survival, maintaining the integrity of character, and earning the king's total trust.

Developing Our Leadership
Exercise 3

Put yourself in the position of being the "turnaround manager" for a declining organization, whether in religion, education, or business. Your task is to lead a narrowly defined project targeted toward tangible results on a limited time schedule with individual or institutional survival at stake. Plan that project by going through the following checklist of competencies learned by Nehemiah in his role as cupbearer for the king.

1. Under what *authority* do you lead?
2. How do you *analyze* the situation under which you must work?
3. What is the felt need that will *activate* your people?
4. How will you *articulate* your plan and command your people?

5. How will you *attend* to detail as a hands-on leader?
6. What internal or external opposition do you *antici-pate?*
7. Is there a potential crisis in the process to which you will have to *adapt?*
8. What are the timely, targeted, and tangible results for which you will be *accountable?*

As you can see from these questions, Nehemiah's experience as a cupbearer prepares him for a hands-on style of leadership in a survival-type situation with quick turnaround on accountability. Are these competencies transferable to a leadership assignment that is larger in scope, more complex in nature, and higher up the scale of human motivation? Nehemiah's call to rebuild the walls of Jerusalem is that kind of challenge.

I devoted myself to the work on this wall (5:16).

—Nehemiah rejects the perks of leadership

Nehemiah's Leadership Journal
Chapters 2:11-20; 4:1—7:2

Nehemiah's Survey
(2:11-16)

I went to Jerusalem, and after staying there three days I set out during the night with a few men. I had not told anyone what God had put in my heart to do for Jerusalem. There were no mounts with me except the one I was riding on.

By night I went out through the Valley Gate toward the Jackal Well and the Dung Gate, examining the walls of Jerusalem, which had been broken down, and its gates, which had been destroyed by fire. Then I moved on toward the Fountain Gate and the King's Pool, but there was not enough room for my mount to get through; so I went up the valley by night, examining the wall. Finally, I turned back and reentered through the Valley Gate. The officials did not know where I had gone or what I was doing, because as yet I had said nothing to the Jews or the priests or nobles or officials or any others who would be doing the work.

Nehemiah's Strategy
(2:17-18)

Then I said to them, "You see the trouble we are in: Jerusalem lies in ruins, and its gates have been burned with fire. Come, let us rebuild the walls of Jerusalem, and we will no longer be in disgrace." I also told them about the gracious hand of my God upon me and what the king had said to me.

They replied, "Let us start rebuilding." So they began this good work.

The Charge of Rebellion
(2:19-20)

But when Sanballat the Horonite, Tobiah the Ammonite official and Geshem the Arab heard about it, they mocked and ridiculed us. "What is this you are doing?" they asked. "Are you rebelling against the king?"

I answered them by saying, "The God of heaven will give us suc-

cess. We his servants will start rebuilding, but as for you, you have no share in Jerusalem or any claim or historic right to it."

Note: An honor roll of the builders of the walls and the gates is recorded in chapter 3 of Nehemiah.

The Laugh of Ridicule
(4:1-3)

When Sanballat heard that we were rebuilding the wall, he became angry and was greatly incensed. He ridiculed the Jews, and in the presence of his associates and the army of Samaria, he said, "What are those feeble Jews doing? Will they restore their wall? Will they offer sacrifices? Will they finish in a day? Can they bring the stones back to life from those heaps of rubble—burned as they are?"

Tobiah the Ammonite, who was at his side, said, "What are they building—even if a fox climbed up on it, he would break down their wall of stones!"

Nehemiah's Response
(4:4-5)

Hear us, O our God, for we are despised. Turn their insults back on their own heads. Give them over as plunder in a land of captivity. Do not cover up their guilt or blot out their sins from your sight, for they have thrown insults in the face of the builders.

Nehemiah's Progress Report
(4:6)

So we rebuilt the wall till all of it reached half its height, for the people worked with all their heart.

The Threat of External Attack
(4:7-9)

But when Sanballat, Tobiah, the Arabs, the Ammonites and the men of Ashdod heard that the repairs to Jerusalem's walls had gone ahead and that the gaps were being closed, they were very angry. They all plotted together to come and fight against

Jerusalem and stir up trouble against it. But we prayed to our God and posted a guard day and night to meet this threat.

Stones and Spears
(4:21-23)

So we continued the work with half the men holding spears, from the first light of dawn till the stars came out. At that time I also said to the people, "Have every man and his helper stay inside Jerusalem at night, so they can serve us as guards by night and workmen by day." Neither I nor my brothers nor my men nor the guards with me took off our clothes; each had his weapon, even when he went for water.

The Threat of Internal Greed
(5:1-5)

Now the men and their wives raised a great outcry against their Jewish brothers. Some were saying, "We and our sons and daughters are numerous; in order for us to eat and stay alive, we must get grain."

Others were saying, "We are mortgaging our fields, our vineyards and our homes to get grain during the famine."

Still others were saying, "We have had to borrow money to pay the king's tax on our fields and vineyards. Although we are of the same flesh and blood as our countrymen and though our sons are as good as theirs, yet we have to subject our sons and daughters to slavery. Some of our daughters have already been enslaved, but we are powerless, because our fields and our vineyards belong to others."

Nehemiah's Angry Action
(5:6-10, 12-13)

When I heard their outcry and these charges, I was very angry. I pondered them in my mind and then accused the nobles and officials. I told them, "You are exacting usury from your own countrymen!" . . . They kept quiet, because they could find nothing to say.

So I continued, "What you are doing is not right. Shouldn't you walk in the fear of our God to avoid the reproach of our Gentile enemies? I and my brothers and my men are also lending the people money and grain. But let the exacting of usury stop!" . . .

"We will give it back," they said. "And we will not demand anything more from them. We will do as you say."

Then I summoned the priests and made the nobles and officials take an oath to do what they had promised. I also shook out the folds of my robe and said, "In this way may God shake out of the house and possessions every man who does not keep this promise. So may such a man be shaken out and emptied!"

At this the whole assembly said, "Amen," and praised the LORD. *And the people did as they had promised.*

Nehemiah's Example
(5:14, 16-19)

Moreover, from the twentieth year of King Artaxerxes, when I was appointed to be their governor in the land of Judah, until his thirty-second year—twelve years—neither I nor my brothers ate the food alloted to the governor. . . . Instead, I devoted myself to the work on this wall. . . .

Furthermore, a hundred and fifty Jews and officials ate at my table, as well as those who came to us from the surrounding nations. . . . I never demanded the food allotted to the governor, because the demands were heavy on these people.

Remember me with favor, O my God, for all I have done for these people.

The Temptation of Compromise
(6:1-4)

When word came to Sanballat, Tobiah, Geshem the Arab and the rest of our enemies that I had rebuilt the wall and not a gap was left in it—though up to that time I had not set the doors in the gates—Sanballat and Geshem sent me this message: "Come, let us meet together in one of the villages on the plain of Ono."

But they were scheming to harm me; so I sent messengers to them with this reply: "I am carrying on a great project and cannot go down. Why should the work stop while I leave it and go down to you?" Four times they sent me the same message, and each time I gave them the same answer.

The Tactic of Treachery
(6:5-9)

Then, the fifth time, Sanballat sent his aide to me with the same message, and in his hand was an unsealed letter in which was written: "It is reported among the nations—and Geshem says it is true—that you and the Jews are plotting to revolt, and therefore you are building the wall. Moreover, according to these reports you are about to become their king and have even appointed prophets to make this proclamation about you in Jerusalem: 'There is a king in Judah.' Now this report will get back to the king; so come, let us confer together." I sent him this reply: "Nothing like what you are saying is happening; you are just making it up out of your head."

They were just trying to frighten us, thinking, "Their hands will get too weak for the work, and it will not be completed." But I prayed, "Now strengthen my hands."

The Threat of Death
(6:10-14)

One day I went to the house of Shemaiah son of Delaiah, the son of Mehetabel, who was shut at his home. He said, "Let us meet in the house of God, inside the temple, and let us close the temple doors, because men are coming to kill you—by night they are coming to kill you."

But I said, "Should a man like me run away? Or should one like me go into the temple to save his life? I will not go!" I realized that God had not sent him, but that he had prophesied against me because Tobiah and Sanballat had hired him. He had been hired to intimidate me so that I would commit a sin by doing this, and then they would give me a bad name to discredit me.

Remember Tobiah and Sanballat, O my God, because of what they have done; remember also the prophetess Noadiah and the rest of the prophets who have been trying to intimidate me.

The Miracle of the Walls
(6:15-16)

So the wall was completed on the twenty-fifth of Elul, in fifty-two days. When all our enemies heard about this, all the sur-

rounding nations were afraid and lost their self-confidence, because they realized that this work had been done with the help of our God.

The Appointment of Gatekeepers (7:1-2)

After the wall had been rebuilt and I had set the doors in place, the gatekeepers and the singers and the Levites were appointed. I put in charge of Jerusalem my brother Hanani, along with Hananiah the commander of the citadel, because he was a man of integrity and feared God more than most men do.

Note: A census of the families of Judah who settled in their hometowns is recorded in chapter 7.

4
THE ENGINEER
LEADERSHIP FOR SECURITY

COME WITH ME now to the second stage in Nehemiah's leadership journey. We move from speculation about his leadership role as the king's man in Susa to an impassioned autobiographical account of his role as God's man in Jerusalem and Israel. From the position as cupbearer of the king assuring good wine for royal meals, he is called to become the engineer of God rebuilding the walls of Jerusalem.

The Call to Lead

The book opens with Nehemiah's memory of the event that is the turning point for his life and the defining moment for his leadership. A delegation of Jews led by Hanani, the brother of Nehemiah, comes from Jerusalem to visit Babylon. Naturally, Nehemiah inquires about the status of the Holy City and his people. He is told that the Jews who survived the exile are demoralized and in disgrace after a hostile attack on the workers who were trying to rebuild the walls and the gates of the city. The holy Temple is still intact, but the Holy City is under imminent threat of destruction.

The Prayer of Preparation

Nehemiah's response lets us look deep into the character of the man. When we speculate about his role as a cupbearer for the king, we assume that he is a person of impeccable integrity, unquestioned loyalty, and mature spirituality. Now we have the facts to back up our assumption. Nehemiah is personally devastated by Hanani's report. With depth of his compassion for his people, he weeps, mourns, fasts, and prays to God:

> O LORD, God of heaven, the great and awesome God, who keeps his covenant of love with those who love him and obey his commands, let your ear be attentive and your eyes open to hear the prayer your servant is praying before you day and night for your servants, the people of Israel. I confess the sins we Israelites, including myself and my father's house, have committed against you. We have acted very wickedly toward you. We have not obeyed the commands, decrees and laws you gave your servant Moses (1:5-7).

This is our model for "The Leader's Prayer of Preparation." Nehemiah is a man who knows what it means to be continually in the presence of the Holy God. He understands the history of Israel, God's covenant of love with His chosen people, and the sins that drove them into Babylonian exile. Even though he is in a powerful position in a pagan land, his first love is the people of God. But most important, even though he has lived a life of utmost integrity in the crucible of the cupbearer, he identifies with the sins of his people in the prayer of confession.

Great leaders invariably demonstrate the gift of knowing the needs of their people and personally identifying with those needs. Mohandas Gandhi, Winston Churchill, Martin Luther King Jr., John Fitzgerald Kennedy, Mother Teresa, Billy Graham—all have made their mark by becoming one with the people they have served. When such people speak, we hear them say, "We." When they act, we see them act for *us*.

Does Nehemiah's prayer give us a key indicator for identifying future leaders for the Church? If leadership begins with compassion for needy people and identification with their needs, we may be looking at leadership development from the wrong end. Passion, vision, creativity, initiative, and charisma are individual gifts we attribute to leaders. Most studies of leadership begin with the individual and these leadership traits. But unless these gifts are matched with urgent needs of distressed people, they become self-serving handicaps of personal ambition. So rather than starting with the individual traits in leadership development, we should start with human needs. Frederick Buechner plumbs the depth of God's heart when he defines our Christian calling as "the place where (our) deep gladness meets the world's deep need" (*Wishful Thinking: A Seeker's ABC* [San Francisco: HarperSanFrancisco, 1993], 119).

At the most fundamental level, we are talking about three human needs cited in the United States Constitution as "life, liberty, and the pursuit of happiness" or the four freedoms that Franklin Delano Roosevelt identified for a democratic society: "Freedom of speech and religion, from want and fear." We may have uncovered an answer to the oft-asked question "Where have all the leaders gone?" For most of the people in our affluent and democratic society, "life and liberty" are no longer basic needs, because we have our life and our liberty. In the same sense, we enjoy the freedoms of speech and religion as well as the freedom from want and fear. Evidence of our freedom from these needs comes forward in the comparison between the driving motives for geeks and geezers. Geezers who grew up in the Great Depression have never lost the haunting memory of "survival needs" in their life experience. Geeks, to the contrary, have never known the gut-level meaning of survival. Their needs for identity and meaning are less fundamental and less desperate than the geezers' needs for survival and security. For this reason alone, it is more difficult to lead geeks than it is to lead geezers. At the very least, the style of leadership must be totally different.

Advance the scale of survival needs into spiritual needs, sensing such as alienation from God, the guilt of sin, and the reality of being lost without faith in Christ, and we begin to understand why the development of Christian leaders is a most difficult task. People for whom life and liberty are guaranteed so that they can concentrate on the pursuit of happiness are those who ask the question, "God? Why do I need Him?" Without a sense of sin and the need for redemption, they are hard to reach and harder to lead.

Over What Do We Weep?

Does Nehemiah's prayer give us a key indicator for identifying future leaders for the Church? We read about Christian leaders of the past weeping, mourning, fasting, and praying for themselves and their people. Is that depth of compassion lost among us today? Has the prayer of confession been sacrificed to the fear that we will be misunderstood if we include ourselves or make our listeners uncomfortable? Much attention is given to spiritual discipline as essential to the development of Christian leaders, but Nehemiah's prayer goes beyond discipline to a broken heart.

Early in my ministry as a Christian leader, I was profoundly influenced by Bob Pierce's book *Let My Heart Be Broken*. As the founder of World Vision, Bob tells about the depth of compassion for the physical, social, and spiritual needs of people, especially for children who were orphaned by the Korean War. Years later, I met Bob at a market square in Lausanne, Switzerland, during the Lausanne Conference on World Evangelization. After we talked for a while, Bob wrapped me in his arms and began to pray. He wept as he confessed our failure to hold the world in our hands and give ourselves unconditionally to its needs. In that unforgettable moment, I felt as if I had my finger on the pulse beat of Christ.

One of the questions we ask when we want to understand the character of an organizational culture is, "Over what do you weep?" Nehemiah gives us a ready answer. He weeps over the plight of his people because of their disobedience to God. Jesus also weeps twice in recorded Scripture. He weeps over the death of His friend Lazarus, and He weeps over His rejection by His people in the Holy City of Jerusalem. We all know what it is to weep over the loss of a human being whom we love, but how many of us have ever wept over a neighborhood, a society, or a nation that has rejected Christ? Over what do we weep? If Christian leadership begins with a broken heart, how many of us really qualify?

Nehemiah's Leadership Challenge

For Nehemiah, the desperate plight of his own people becomes the call of God to a very specific task of rebuilding the walls of Jerusalem. Will the skills he learned as a cupbearer to the king transfer to a massive construction project in a distant land with limited resources and dispirited workers?

Nehemiah immediately puts his learning from the crucible into action as a leader. The crisis in Jerusalem is a match for the key competencies of a cupbearer. Not all leadership competencies are transferable from one situation to another. Only the competencies of character apply in every situation. Whatever his leadership role, we can count on Nehemiah being a man of integrity, loyalty, prayer, and self-sacrifice. In leadership development we often say, "Past performance is the best predictor of future performance." It is generally true, but we need to add the caveat that it depends upon the similarity of the situation. A pastor may transfer skill sets from parish to parish, but they may not transfer to the mission field, an educational institution, or a denominational office. In Nehemiah's case, the skill set of the cupbearer transfers to the rebuilding of the walls of Jerusalem. For this narrow, focused, and timely task, God needs an engineer.

Transferable Skills

Nehemiah begins by seeking authority for his task. As a man who understands the power of authority, he realizes that he cannot rely alone upon the inferred authority of his character or the earned authority of his past success. For the urgent task of rebuilding the walls, he needs an all-powerful authority that everyone knows and obeys. Because Jerusalem is the province of Artaxerxes, Nehemiah seeks the ascribed authority conferred by the king. Nehemiah's face shows both the depth of his distress and the height of his anxiety in his next meeting with the king. The palace is a paranoidal place. To show a downcast look in the presence of the king is to raise suspicion of conspiracy and put your life at risk. Yet because Nehemiah has earned the trust of the king, Artaxerxes asks, "What is wrong?" Nehemiah answers by telling his story and asking for the privilege of a leave of absence to go home and rebuild the walls. God has gone before His obedient servant. In answer to his prayers, the king grants Nehemiah a leave of absence from his role as cupbearer along with assurance of safe conduct through 700 miles of enemy territory on his way home. Just in case, the royal guard of the king will be his escort. No one dares dis-

obey or touch Nehemiah without invoking the wrath of Artaxerxes himself. Even though critics in Jerusalem might see
him as a carpetbagger, Nehemiah will carry the clout of E. F.
Hutton—when he speaks, everyone listens.

*Next, Nehemiah requests the authority for resources to rebuild
the gates of Jerusalem.* Boldness follows boldness in the development of leadership. In contemporary parlance, Nehemiah
knows that a startup or turnaround project requires "Father's
love" and "Mother's milk." "Father's love" is the passionate
commitment of leadership to the task, and "Mother's milk"
represents the resources necessary to bring it to completion.
Nehemiah has the passion of a father's love for the project
but comes up short on resources. Stones in the rubble are
enough to rebuild the walls, but he lacks the wood to rebuild
the burned-out gates and construct a home for himself.
Knowing that he cannot make bricks without straw or build
gates without wood, he asks the king to provide him with all
the wood he needs from the royal forest. In response to this
request, the king gives him a voucher to assure the wood
needed to rebuild the gates of the city.

After the 700-mile journey through the wilderness from
Babylon to Jerusalem, Nehemiah arrives safely in Jerusalem
ready to work. Opposition has already arisen from Sanballat
and Tobiah, who want to keep the Jews vulnerable to their
attack and under their control. So after resting for just three
days, *Nehemiah puts his analytical skills to work, surveying the
scene and preparing his plan.* Under cover of night, he climbs
over the rubble of the ruins and views the charred remains
of the gates. He knows that he must act fast. Dividing the
monstrous project into manageable tasks with measurable
outcomes along the way, Nehemiah now has a plan to go
with his authority and his resources.

The next step is to articulate the plan so that it has meaning for people. From his days as a cupbearer to the king, Nehemiah knows that survival is the deepest of human motives. Without the walls and the gates, neither Jerusalem nor the Jews can survive.

John Hershey, author of *Hiroshima,* wrote a book titled *Here to Stay,* in which he tells unbelievable stories of human survival, including that of John F. Kennedy swimming through the night around a small Pacific island after his PT boat was shot out from under him, and that of a woman in her 80s traveling hand over hand on a rope several stories in the air in order to escape the famous Johnstown, Pennsylvania, flood.

Nehemiah appeals to this same survival instinct. Although he has dictatorial authority, adequate resources, and a realistic plan to build the walls, he cannot succeed as a leader without the full commitment of the people. Does the situation sound familiar? The terrorists of September 11, 2001, drove Americans back to the survival motive. George W. Bush became their leader as well as their president when he identified with their pain, put the face of evil on the enemy, and launched a counterattack. Americans rallied to his call and even allowed restrictions to their freedom in order to assure survival.

Nehemiah wins the same kind of support. Everyone in the city becomes a hod-carrier, a stonecutter, or a mason during those days. Family feuds are put aside, priests and people work together, rich and poor forget their differences, goldsmiths and perfume-makers get their hands dirty, and rulers join with the masses to rebuild the walls. Only some spoiled nobles refuse to work.

In the contemporary language of team-building, Nehemiah gets the right people on the bus, the wrong people off the bus, and the right people in the right seats (James Collins, *Good to Great* [New York: HarperCollins, 2001], 184). With this stroke of organizational genius, Nehemiah turns a ragtag army into a unified and potent construction crew.

Halfway through the project, when fatigue is taking its toll on the builders, Nehemiah's skills of leadership undergo another test. Sanballat and Tobiah seize the moment to strike at the morale of the people by ridiculing their work and then plotting an attack against the builders. Out of desperate prayer, Nehemiah shows his genius. Organizing the builders by families and dividing the ranks of men into those holding spears and those working trowels, he staves off the threat and further frustrates Sanballat and Tobiah.

Having failed with the roar of the lion, Sanballat and Tobiah try the cooing of the dove. When they do, they play right into the strength of Nehemiah. *As the cupbearer of the king, he knows how to anticipate conspiracy.* Four times they try to get Nehemiah to stop working and meet with them in a summit meeting. Knowing their scheme, he refuses each time. On the fifth try, then, they reveal their hand when they spread the rumor that the Jews are rebuilding the walls so that they can rebel against Artaxerxes and make Nehemiah their king. Again, they fail when Nehemiah calls their bluff.

As a last resort, they try to cower Nehemiah with the threat of assassination. Bribing a friend of Nehemiah, they propose that he save his life and his leadership by hiding himself within the Temple where assassins cannot go. Once again, crying out to God for new strength, Nehemiah goes back to work at the risk of his life.

One thinks of Winston Churchill striding over the rubble of London and growling, "We have just begun to fight!"

Nehemiah knows that his personal presence and his hands-on, hard labor are needed to finish the job. And so in just 52 days the walls are up and the gates are hung. Jerusalem is secure, and the people are safe.

What a feat of engineering! It is like the Eiffel Tower in Paris. It began as a vision in the mind of the builder and subject to the ridicule of those who said it couldn't be done. They predicted that the tower would topple from the winds or crumble under the shock of an earthquake. The builder, however, took the challenge and designed the structure with openings in the girders to withstand the wind and complementary tensions to survive an earthquake. In a statuesque rebuff to their critics, the Eiffel Tower still stands. In like fashion, Nehemiah's wall withstood all the buffeting of the elements. Only the siege of enemies could bring the wall down.

Prayers of Engagement

Go back a moment to the prayers of Nehemiah during the engineering stage. He records no prayers during the early stages of the building. Sometimes we are too busy to pray. In those times, it is the prayer capital we invested over a long period of time upon which we can bank. Brother Andrew in his classic book *Practicing His Presence* reminds us that we can be in the spirit of prayer and in the presence of God while doing dishes in the kitchen. But when strength begins to fail and conspiracies threaten, Nehemiah knows that his God will give him strength and keep him safe. Like old friends who meet after a prolonged absence, Nehemiah and God can start the conversation right where they left off. *These are the prayers of engagement—short, intense, and urgent.* "Now, strengthen my hands" is the prayer of a leader at work.

Lessons from the Engineer

What leadership lessons do we learn from Nehemiah's role as an engineer? For one thing, *we learn that God uses the crucible of experience as a time of preparation for a selected task.* Both character and competence are shaped in that defining moment. While the qualities of character transfer to any leadership role, the skills of competence are honed for a special task.

For another thing, *we learn that leadership comes in many skill sets that apply to specific situations.* Nehemiah shows us how an engineering mind works. Backed up by the king's authority, he analyzes the situation, articulates a plan, attends to detail, and accepts accountability for the project. In current parlance, Nehemiah would probably be described as an authoritarian micromanager capitalizing on the motive of self-survival, but that's the kind of leadership required to rebuild the walls in 52 days. He succeeds, not just because of his spiritual depth and his personal integrity but also because of the adapting of his competencies to match the needs of the project. For those who insist that entrepreneurship is synonymous with leadership, Nehemiah will be a disappointment. He is not an entrepreneur with a lofty vision taking a giant risk; rather, he is an engineer with a practical task working a predetermined plan. God does not play favorites.

Give Nehemiah another credit in leadership development. *He understands the advanced level of motivation needed for the people to rebuild the walls.* As cupbearer to the king, he deals with the most basic of human needs, the need to stay alive. Although the inhabitants of Jerusalem have faced threat after threat to their survival, they have succeeded in rebuilding the Temple and establishing their homes. Their need now is security or freedom from fear. Nehemiah knows that the rebuilding of the walls will give them freedom from that fear. If he can complete the urgent task in a timely fashion, more than walls will be built—his people will again gain self-esteem as God's chosen people.

Nehemiah also shows us the adaptability required to meet a new challenge. Under the iron fist of King Artaxerxes, every subject of the realm is obedient to the king's command. There are no options. Either you obey or you die. Nehemiah succeeds under the authority of that regime, but he is not bound by it. When he goes to Jerusalem under the call of God to rebuild the walls, he has to deal with people who have options. Perhaps for the first time Nehemiah learns what it means to work with volunteers. How will he motivate the people of Jerusalem to work day and night in order to rebuild the walls? His answer is a stroke of genius. Knowing the tight lines that bind tribes, families, and occupations together, he appeals to each of these relationships as the incentive for selfless work. He chunks the work into manageable bits, keeps the labor close to home, and wins the day. Although the step is small, Nehemiah shows genius for adaptability.

The church is also an army of volunteers. To lead them is like herding a litter of kittens. They go every-which way. Nehemiah, however, gives us some hope. To lead volunteers, we need to *motivate* them by their felt needs, *mobilize* them by their interpersonal relationships, *organize* them by manageable tasks, *reward* them by tangible results, and *encourage* them by working the hardest of all. Thank you, Nehemiah.

Developing Our Leadership
Exercise 4

Put yourself into a leadership situation in which success

depends upon the effectiveness of volunteers, such as organizing small-group ministries. Following Nehemiah's example, ask yourself these questions:

- What is the felt need that *motivates* them?
- What is the relational connection that *mobilizes* them?
- Who are the natural leaders to *supervise* them?
- What is the manageable task that *energizes* them?
- What are the tangible results that *reward* them?
- What is the personal proof of your *commitment* to them?

Volunteer ministries, such as small groups, often fail. Out
of your experience, which item from the questions above is
most critical to their success, and where do we fail?

I was appointed to be their governor in the land of Judah (5:14).

—Nehemiah's advancement to executive position

Nehemiah's Leadership Journal
Chapters 7:73—10:39; 12:27-43

Rebuilding the Nation
(7:73—8:2, 5-6)

When the seventh month came and the Israelites had settled into their towns, all the people assembled as one man in the square before the Water Gate. They told Ezra the scribe to bring out the Book of the Law of Moses, which the LORD had commanded for Israel.

So on the first day of the seventh month Ezra the priest brought the Law before the assembly, which was made up of men and women and all who were able to understand. . . . Ezra opened the book. All the people could see him because he was standing above them; and as he opened it, the people all stood up. Ezra praised the LORD, the great God; and all the people lifted their hands and responded, "Amen! Amen!" Then they bowed down and worshiped the LORD with their faces to the ground.

Nehemiah's Proclamation
(8:9-10)

Then Nehemiah the governor, Ezra the priest and scribe, and the Levites who were instructing the people said to them all, "This day is sacred to the LORD your God. Do not mourn or weep." For all the people had been weeping as they listened to the words of the Law.

Nehemiah said, "Go and enjoy choice food and sweet drinks, and send some to those who have nothing prepared. This day is sacred to our Lord. Do not grieve, for the joy of the LORD is your strength."

A Feast Restored
(8:13-18)

On the second day of the month, the heads of all the families, along with the priests and the Levites, gathered around Ezra the scribe to give attention to the words of the Law. They found written in the Law, which the LORD had commanded through Moses, that the Israelites were to live in booths during the feast of the seventh month and that they should proclaim this word and spread it throughout their towns and in Jerusalem: "Go out into the hill country and bring back branches from olive and wild olive trees, and from myrtles, palms and shade trees, to make booths" —as it is written.

So the people went out and brought back branches and built themselves booths on their own roofs, in their courtyards, in the courts of the house of God and in the square by the Water Gate and the one by the Gate of Ephraim. The whole company that had returned from exile built booths and lived in them. From the days of Joshua son of Nun until that day, the Israelites had not celebrated it like this. And their joy was very great.

Day after day, from the first day to the last, Ezra read from the Book of the Law of God. They celebrated the feast for seven days, and on the eighth day, in accordance with the regulation, there was an assembly.

Israel's Confession of Sin
(9:1-3, 36-37)

On the twenty-fourth day of the same month, the Israelites gathered together, fasting and wearing sackcloth and having dust on their heads. Those of Israelite descent had separated them- selves from all foreigners. They stood in their places and con- fessed their sins and the wickedness of their fathers. They stood where they were and read from the Book of the Law of the Lord their God for a quarter of the day, and spent another quarter in confession and in worshiping the Lord their God.

Note: The Israelites' prayer of confession follows in 9:5-37 with this conclusion:

But see, we are slaves today, slaves in the land you gave our forefathers so they could eat its fruit and the other good things it produces. Because of our sins, its abundant harvest goes to the kings you have placed over us. They rule over our bodies and our cattle as they please. We are in great distress.

A New Commitment
(9:38; 10:30-32, 35, 37, 39)

In view of all this, we are making a binding agreement, putting it in writing, and our leaders, our Levites and our priests are affixing their seals to it. . . .

We promise not to give our daughters in marriage to the peoples around us or take their daughters for our sons.

When the neighboring peoples bring merchandise or grain to sell on the Sabbath, we will not buy from them on the Sabbath or on any holy day. Every seventh year, we will forgo working the land and will cancel all debts.

We assume the responsibility to carry out the commands to give a third of a shekel each year for the service of the house of our God. . . .

We also assume responsibility for bringing to the house of the LORD each year the firstfruits of our crops and of every fruit tree. . . .

Moreover, we will bring to the storerooms of the house of our God, to the priests, the first of our ground meal, of our grain offerings, of the fruit of all our trees and of our new wine and oil. And we will bring a tithe of our crops to the Levites, for it is the Levites who collect the tithes in all the towns where we work. . . .

We will not neglect the house of our God.

Note: The resettlement of the people in Jerusalem and the towns throughout Judea is recorded in 11:1—12:26.

Dedication of the Wall
(12:27-28, 30-31; 38, 40-43)

At the dedication of the wall of Jerusalem, the Levites were sought out from where they lived and were brought to Jerusalem to celebrate joyfully the dedication with songs of thanksgiving and with the music of cymbals, harps and lyres. The singers also were brought together from the region around Jerusalem. . . . When the priests and Levites had purified themselves ceremonially, they purified the people, the gates and the wall.

I had the leaders of Judah go up on top of the wall. I also assigned two large choirs to give thanks. One was to proceed on top of the wall to the right, toward the Dung Gate. . . . The second choir proceeded in the opposite direction. I followed them on top of the wall, together with half the people. . . . The two choirs that gave thanks then took their places in the house of God; so did I, together with half the officials, as well as the priests. . . .

The choirs sang under the direction of Jezrahiah. And on that day they offered great sacrifices, rejoicing because God had given them great joy. The women and children also rejoiced. The sound of rejoicing in Jerusalem could be heard far away.

5
THE GOVERNOR
LEADERSHIP FOR SIGNIFICANCE

WITH THE COMPLETION of the walls assured, Nehemiah is appointed governor of the province of Jerusalem in the 20th year of King Artaxerxes. All the dimensions of Nehemiah's leadership change. The scale of his responsibility grows from that of rebuilding the walls of Jerusalem to that of rebuilding the nation. The scope of his duties expands from that of addressing the urgent need for security to that of the longer-term need for significance. The complexity of his role moves from the physical task of rebuilding the walls to the more ambiguous arena of public policy, local politics, and international relations. Certainly, his personal integrity and spiritual depth will transfer to this new responsibility, but what about the competencies of the cupbearer and the engineer?

Rebuilding the Nation

Is Nehemiah up to the task? Or is the Peter Principle at work? Has he been promoted to his level of incompetence? Another crucible awaits him as he takes on the duties of rebuilding a nation after his success in rebuilding the walls.

The walls give the Jews a measure of security, but the Jews lack unity as a people and respect as a nation. Rebuilding the structure of a nation becomes the large, long-term, and far more difficult task facing Nehemiah, the governor. Spiritual, social, and political rubble lies at his feet.

Nehemiah responds by *reestablishing the moral and legal foun-*

dation upon which the nation will be built. Gathering all the people at the Water Gate, he calls in Ezra, the priest, for the reading of the Law. As they see these two together on a public platform, the crowd witnesses the symbol of spiritual and secular leadership coming together around the commandments and the covenant of God. A comparable act in the United States would be our leaders calling us together for a reading of the Constitution and the Ten Commandments!

When the people hear the reading of the Law and realize how far they have gone astray, they weep and mourn. Nehemiah, however, tells them that it is not the time to mourn but *the time to celebrate their newfound freedom with singing and feasting.* Every nation needs its Fourth of July. Out of the Jews' celebration comes the Feast of Tabernacles or Booths as a lasting reminder of their deliverance from bondage in Egypt as well as Babylon.

Nehemiah then presents a binding agreement *signed and sealed by all the people, beginning with himself, as a national commitment to obey all God's commands, regulations, and decrees.* Again, every nation needs a code of conduct, not unlike our Bill of Rights, with which everyone agrees and obeys. In this case, the Jews agree not to compromise their faith, intermarry with surrounding nations, buy and sell on the Sabbath, neglect the house of the Lord by failing to contribute their tithe, or forget their responsibility for sustaining the priesthood.

With the foundation of the Law, the holy day for celebration, and signed agreement to obey God, the nation-building continues as Nehemiah *appoints leaders over the city of Jerusalem and the towns of the province.* Resettlement takes place as some volunteers stay in Jerusalem while their families return to their hometowns. Nehemiah's gift for motivating and organizing people serves him well once again. Because he has been consistent in his leadership while rebuilding the walls, his followers know they can trust him.

One more pillar is needed for the foundation of the nation. *Nehemiah restores the national treasury.* Economic security is another symbol of significance among the competing nations of the Middle East. Notably, Nehemiah personally makes the first and largest gift. His act indicates the wealth he has accumulated as a cupbearer to the king. More significantly, it symbolizes his total commitment to his people and the leadership example for others to follow. In a companion move of equal import, Nehemiah scorches the nobles and officials who are robbing the poor by taxing them so heavily that they have to exhaust their cash in order to eat, sell their daughters into slavery to pay their debts, and mortgage their lands in order to survive. Losing their freedom from want, they have become the slaves of their own brethren. With unbridled anger, Nehemiah orders full restitution of the money to the poor and extracts the promise from the haughty nobles and the corrupt officials that it will never happen again. Then, to balance his act of anger, Nehemiah sets the example by refusing to take the governor's generous allotment for food to feed himself and his staff because the funds have come from the taxes on poor people.

I have a friend who was the political editor for a local newspaper. His weekly column became known as the watchdog on the integrity of state and local politicians. At lunch one day, he gave me the rule under which he worked to monitor the character of political leaders. He said, "Check their financial assets when they enter office and when they leave. You'll know immediately whether they're honest or corrupt." Integrity of leadership shows itself in many forms, but financial integrity is the telltale indicator.

Once the pillars of nationhood are in place and the resettlement is done, *Nehemiah calls the people back for the dedication of the walls, which symbolize their newfound nationhood.* Physical walls represent their security; moral and spiritual principles lift them to significance. It is time for singers to give thanks as they lead the way along the top of the walls with Nehemiah following behind. Gatekeepers are officially installed into their positions, and the priests preside over the process of purifying and filling the storerooms of the Temple as commanded by God. Nehemiah's exuberance rings through his words "The sound of rejoicing in Jerusalem could be heard far away" (12:43). In each instance, the character and competencies of the crucible continue to come through. Nehemiah is more than a wall-builder—he is a nation-builder as well.

Leadership Lessons from the Governor

Nehemiah moves to maturity in his leadership as governor of the city of Jerusalem and the province of Israel. Rebuilding a nation that is ridiculed as a "worm under the feet" of hostile neighbors and restoring the confidence of a demoralized people are formidable tests of his leadership. But Nehemiah is up to the challenge. He responds with qualities of leadership that can be applied to the founding or renewal of any nation, institution, or organization. Christian leaders in particular will find ready application of Nehemiah's leadership qualities in their own ministries.

Showing strong evidence of his maturity in leadership development, *Nehemiah adapts his style to changes in his situation.* As the cupbearer for the king with physical survival at stake, he exercises tight control over the process and the people under his command. As the engineer of God rebuilding the walls of Jerusalem to give the inhabitants security from attack, he earns the authority of command by his planning, organization, operation, and hands-on labor. Governorship, however, requires a major adjustment in leadership style. Nehemiah must shift from the control of process and command of people to *collaboration involving policy, politics, and public opinion*. If Nehemiah had persisted in his leadership style as a cupbearer or an engineer, he would have failed as a governor.

Effective leaders, especially those who serve long-term, flex in style as the situation changes. This does not mean a compromise of morals or principles. In the language of James McGregor Burns, a transactional leader can be just as effective as a transformational leader. In fact, the same leader may be transformational at one time and transactional at another time. Nehemiah shows how to be both. As a cupbearer, he exhibits leadership that is almost exclusively transactional. As an engineer, however, he has a vision in his plans to rebuild the walls, a vision that is beginning to take on the characteristics of transformation. In his governorship, the scale is tipped heavily toward a transforming style that lifts a nation into significance. Nehemiah illustrates the fact that great leaders cannot be stereotyped by style. In the crucible of experience, they learn to adapt to changing circumstances without losing their personal integrity.

Nehemiah shows us another quality of maturity in his understanding of what it will take to rebuild the nation. His first decision is to call Ezra, the scribe, into coleadership with him. Even though Nehemiah has the glow of success in rebuilding the walls and the clout of the king's authority, he knows that the rebuilding of the nation depends upon a legal, moral, and spiritual foundation. Ezra is the expert in this field. Day after day, Ezra reads The Law of the Book of Moses to the people, recalling the fact that God has given them "regulations and laws that are just and right, and decrees and commands that are good." (9:13). It is a declaration of independence for Israel. The people respond with prayers of confession followed by feasts of rejoicing and the restoration of the Festival of the Booths as symbols of their newfound freedom.

Once Ezra's reading of the Book of Moses is complete, *Nehemiah leads the way in signing and sealing a binding agreement to obey the letter and the spirit of the Law.* Every priest in Israel and the head of every family throughout the land follows suit. Signed and sealed into a common commitment, the agreement serves as a constitution for nationhood. Included in their commitment are such fundamentals actions as restoring the Sabbath principle, revering the House of God, rejecting mixed marriages, rebuilding of the national treasury, and providing for the needs of the clergy.

One more foundational stone has to be laid for the rebuilding of the nation. Jews who cower behind the security of the walls of Jerusalem need to be resettled in the towns and villages of Israel as evidence of their confidence in God's promise for His people. For further assurance, Nehemiah appoints a full complement of *provincial leaders* for every town and village in the land. The network of religious, secular, and family relationships is now complete. Every Israelite has a personal role in rebuilding the nation.

Nehemiah adds to the evidence of his growth when he deals effectively with paradox in his leadership. In his earlier assignments, he faced black-and-white issues. There were no ambiguities in the responsibility of a cupbearer and few complications in the role of an engineer. But as governor, Nehemiah steps into a political arena where ambiguity reigns and paradox rules. So his work is not done. As a leader, he faces the dilemma of balancing confession with celebration, weeping with singing, and religious reform with spiritual renewal. His task is like that of a school administrator who has responsibility for both discipline and counseling, or a prison official who is held accountable for both custody and rehabilitation. As tough as it is, paradox is the test of leadership.

Nehemiah especially agonizes over the tough decisions he has to make as a *reformer*. He purges heathens from the House of God, orders the people to bring tithes and offerings into the storehouse as provisions for the priests, throws out merchants who violate the Sabbath, reprimands men who marry pagan wives, and purifies the priesthood from foreign elements. His decisions range from surgical decisions to angry expulsions. Both actions go against his nature, because he follows every disciplinary act with a prayer asking God to remember him for doing what he knows he must do. Yet this is the lot of leadership. For the higher and greater good, a leader suffers the agony and loneliness of painful decisions.

As final proof of Nehemiah's maturity as a leader, we learn that he is a master of symbols. Once the walls are rebuilt and the foundation of the nation is reestablished, it is time to celebrate the work with a ceremony of dedication. Nehemiah takes the lead in planning a program that features the songs of choirs and music of instruments. All the priests and choirs from the towns and villages are called back to Jerusalem for a national day of dedication. Symbolically, Nehemiah calls all of the leaders to the top of the wall, puts the choirs out in front, and takes his place behind them. It is a master stroke as all the people rejoice and "The sound of rejoicing in Jerusalem could be heard far away" (12:43). Friends and enemies who hear the singing know that Jerusalem is secure and that Israel has taken a place of significance among nations.

The dedication of the walls reminds us of other events in which Nehemiah showed his mastery of symbols for communication. His midnight walk over the rubble of the walls signifies his personal identification with the needs of the people so that he can gather the leaders of the city together and rally them to work. Equally powerful is his hands-on labor, which becomes a model of self-deployment for priests, artisans, and heads of families to follow. In contrast to the nobles who refuse to join the work, Nehemiah undoubtedly wins the hearts of the people. Later, as the work is going on, Nehemiah finds out that the same nobles and officials who refuse to work are gouging the poor by charging exorbitant interest on personal loans and mortgages on land. When the charge comes to Nehemiah's attention, he commands the priests, nobles, and public officials to come to a meeting and sign an oath pledging that they will return the money and stop the practice. But when he shakes out the folds of his robes as a symbol of God's wrath and the king's authority, the action speaks loud and clear. Best of all, however, is the defiance of Nehemiah when the conspirators Sanballat and Geshem send him an invitation to stop his work and come down from the wall in order to attend a meeting in which they can allegedly settle their differences. Four times their flattering invitation comes, and four times Nehemiah refuses it, saying, "I am carrying on a great project and cannot go down. Why should the work stop while I leave it and go down to you?" (6:3) As word of his reply spreads among the builders, who are totally exhausted but within days of completing the work, their fatigue gives way to a burst of energy that drives them forward. With the inspiration of Nehemiah's refusal to stop the work for the sake of flattery, the walls are finished in a record time of 52 days. Great leaders are masters of symbols in communicating their vision to energize and mobilize the masses.

So as governor of Judah, Nehemiah shows us how a leader grows as he or she goes. The leader adapts his or her style of leadership to changing circumstances, shares his or her authority to rebuild the nation on the foundation of Moses' Law and God's covenant, makes decisions for the greater good at a personal cost, and masters the symbols of communication. Nehemiah is a candidate for greatness among leaders who reform and renew our social institutions upon sound legal, moral, and spiritual grounds.

Developing Our Leadership
Exercise 5

Vision is the major emphasis in leadership development today. A visionary leader, however, must also be a foundational leader who builds and renews an organization on sound historical, legal, moral, and spiritual principles. Nehemiah shows us how these principles are applied to the restoration of Israel as a nation of significance. Do the same principles apply to building and renewing your ministry?

1. Are the *historical and legal grounds* of your organization documented in writing and understood by all members?

2. Are the *moral standards* for judging right and wrong behavior clear to all members and accepted by them?

3. Are the *spiritual expectations* a vital part of the organizational culture, with all members contributing to their fulfillment?

4. How do the members *sign and seal their commitment* to these principles?

Now advance the questions to your leadership of the organization.

1. What does your organization *celebrate?* How do you lead the celebration?
2. What are the *paradoxes* with which you have to deal in your organization? How have you tried to resolve them?
3. What *symbols* do you use to communicate the mission and meaning of your organization to its members?

By asking the same questions that Nehemiah asked, we may well find the answer to rebuilding, reforming, and renewing our ministry.

But while all of this was going on, I was not in Jerusalem (13:6).

—Nehemiah's despair when he learns that his reforms have failed

Nehemiah's Leadership Journal
Chapter 13

Corruption in the House of God
(13:1, 3)

On that day the Book of Moses was read aloud in the hearing of the people and there it was found written that no Ammonite or Moabite should ever be admitted into the assembly of God. . . . When the people heard this law, they excluded from Israel all who were of foreign descent.

The Cause of Corruption
(13:4-5)

Before this, Eliashib the priest had been put in charge of the storerooms of the house of our God. He was closely associated with Tobiah [the Ammonite], and he had provided him with a large room formerly used to store the grain offerings and incense and temple articles, and also the tithes of grain, new wine and oil pre-scribed for the Levites, singers and gatekeepers, as well as the contributions for the priests.

Nehemiah's Reforms
(13:6-9)

But while all this was going on, I was not in Jerusalem, for in the thirty-second year of Artaxerxes king of Babylon I had re-turned to the king. Some time later I asked his permission and came back to Jerusalem. Here I learned about the evil thing Eliashib had done in providing Tobiah a room in the courts of the house of God.

I was greatly displeased and threw all Tobiah's household goods out of the room. I gave orders to purify the rooms, and then I put back into them the equipment of the house of God, with the grain offerings and the incense.

Restoring the Tithes
(13:10-14)

I also learned that the portions assigned to the Levites had

not been given to them, and that all the Levites and singers re-
sponsible for the service had gone back to their own fields. So I
rebuked the officials and asked them, "Why is the house of God
neglected?" Then I called them together and stationed them at
their posts.

All Judah brought the tithes of grain, new wine and oil into the
storerooms. I put Shelemiah the priest, Zadok the scribe, and a
Levite named Pedaiah in charge of the storerooms and made
Hanan son of Zaccur, the son of Mattaniah, their assistant, be-
cause these men were considered trustworthy. . . .

Remember me for this, O my God, and do not blot out what I
have so faithfully done for the house of my God and its services.

Honoring the Sabbath
(13:15-19, 22)

In those days I saw men in Judah treading winepresses on the
Sabbath and bringing in grain and loading it on donkeys, together
with wine, grapes, figs and all other kinds of loads. And they were
bringing all this into Jerusalem on the Sabbath. Therefore I warned
them against selling food on that day. Men from Tyre who lived in
Jerusalem were bringing in fish and all kinds of merchandise and
selling them in Jerusalem on the Sabbath to the people of Judah.
I rebuked the nobles of Judah and said to them, "What is this
wicked thing you are doing—desecrating the Sabbath day? Didn't
your forefathers do the same things, so that our God brought all
this calamity upon us and upon this city? Now you are stirring up
more wrath against Israel by desecrating the Sabbath."

When evening shadows fell on the gates of Jerusalem before the
Sabbath, I ordered the doors to be shut and not opened until the
Sabbath was over. . . . Then I commanded the Levites to purify
themselves and go and guard the gates in order to keep the Sab-
bath day holy. Remember me for this also, O my God, and show
mercy to me according to your great love.

Sanctifying Marriage
(13:23-27)

Moreover, in those days I saw men of Judah who had married
women from Ashdod, Ammon and Moab. Half of their children

spoke the language of Ashdod or the language of one of the oth-er peoples, and did not know how to speak the language of Ju-dah. I rebuked them and called curses down on them. I beat some of the men and pulled out their hair. I made them take an oath in God's name and said: "You are not to give your daughters in marriage to their sons, nor are you to take their daughters in marriage for your sons or for yourselves. Was it not because of marriages like these that Solomon king of Israel sinned? Among the many nations there was no king like him. He was loved by his God, and God made him king over all Israel, but even he was led into sin by foreign women. Must we hear now that you too are do-ing all this terrible wickedness and are being unfaithful to our God by marrying foreign women?"

Purifying the Priesthood
(13:28-31)

One of the sons of Joiada son of Eliashib the high priest was son-in-law to Sanballat the Horonite. And I drove him away from me.

Remember them, O my God, because they have defiled the priestly office and the covenant of the priesthood and of the Levites.

So I purified the priests and the Levites of everything foreign, and assigned them duties, each to his own task. I also made pro-vision for contributions of wood at designated times, and for the firstfruits.

Remember me with favor, O my God.

6
THE STATESMAN
LEADERSHIP FOR SUCCESSION

NEHEMIAH'S JOURNEY does not end here. An unexpected test of his leadership comes when his leave of absence from the court of the king expires and he has to return to Babylon. He is still governor of the province, but in the role of an absentee landlord. Here is where the trouble begins. Before he leaves Jerusalem, he puts Eliashib, the priest, in charge of the Temple storerooms. He trusts him even though he knows that he is closely associated with Tobiah, the devious man who has been Nehemiah's nemesis from the very beginning. When Nehemiah gets the king's permission to return to Jerusalem for his second term, he learns that Tobiah has been given a storeroom in the house of God. The Temple is now corrupted, the priests are neglected, and the singing stops. From here on, Nehemiah has to assume the role of a "turnaround" manager. His career closes with him acting angrily, not just against Tobiah but against all the leaders who have lapsed from the code of conduct by corrupting the House of God, neglecting the priesthood, buying and selling on the Sabbath, and intermarrying with pagan neighbors.

Prayers of Remembrance

Nehemiah's prayers reflect his distaste for this new role. He turns inward with prayers of remembrance, pleading with God for favor because of his aggressive acts to counter corruption. Venting his anger against Eliashib, he throws all

of Tobiah's furnishings out of the storeroom in the Temple.
Then he threatens to manhandle the men who desecrate
the Sabbath. For the men of Judah who marry foreign wives,
he curses them, beats some of them, and tears their hair out.
After each act, he prays a prayer that the Jewish Bible inter-
prets as "O my God, remember me with credit."

In his book *Good to Great* James Collins draws the distinc-
tion between good and great leaders on this point. A great
leader, according to Collins, will look into the mirror for
blame and out the window for credit (33). Nehemiah does
the opposite. By looking in the mirror for credit and out the
window for blame, he loses the edge of greatness to which he
has risen. Suddenly the singing stops, the joy is gone, and we
hear the plaintive cry of a leader who is acting out of character and feeling as if all his work is in vain. Nehemiah's words
haunt us when he sums up his life and ends his book with
words that he has spoken four times in the final stage of his
career, "Remember me with favor, O my God" (13:31). Always before, he let his works speak for themselves.

The Turning Point

What is the turning point in Nehemiah's leadership journey that leaves him pleading to be remembered by God? The
clue is in his appointment of Eliashib, a close friend of Tobiah, his archenemy. No sooner is Nehemiah out of town than
Eliashib gives Tobiah a large storeroom in the House of God
where articles of worship are kept along with the tithes of
grain, wine, and oil as provision for the priests, singers, and
gatekeepers. By giving the space to Tobiah, Eliashib corrupts
the Temple, violates his constitutional commitment, and ne-
glects the House of God. Because of this action, worship ceas-
es, singing stops, and the gates are left unprotected. All the

work that Nehemiah has done to rebuild the nation stands in jeopardy. So when he returns from Babylon, he spends the rest of his known career as a turnaround manager wielding a sharp ax with angry words and volatile actions. He reaches a fever pitch when he confronts the men who have married pagan wives. In his own words, Nehemiah says, "I rebuked them and called curses down on them. I beat some of the men and pulled out their hair" (13:25). It is no surprise that he follows with the plaintive plea "Remember me with favor, O God." Futility echoes through his words, and resentment is read between the lines.

Twelve years of great accomplishment are wiped out, and in the final years of his governance, Nehemiah is relegated once again to the detestable work of cleaning house. With the same kind of anger that Job voices against God for his suffering, Nehemiah is complaining about his lot in leadership. He fears that he will be remembered for his rash acts of moral and spiritual reform, not as the governor who rebuilt the walls, restored the nation, and renewed the covenant with God. Behind his appeal for remembrance is the hidden thought *God, I followed your call and tried to do your will, but look where it has taken me. Remember me with favor.* Self-doubt rules, and self-pity reigns. Will the leadership of Nehemiah end under a shadow?

A Perspective on the Problem

Every honest leader will identify with Nehemiah. The journey of leadership is not a freeway without speed bumps. Praise is countered by criticism, confidence is tempered by doubt, success is matched by failure, spectacles are followed by dullness, and singing gives way to sadness. But as Nehemiah finds, nothing is more distressing than to feel as if all our work is in vain. What happens to Nehemiah? We need to look deeper into the final chapter of his career in order to understand him and gain a perspective on his leadership in total, not in part.

There is no doubt that Nehemiah makes a bad decision that comes back to haunt him. When his sabbatical is over and he must return to Babylon, he puts Eliashib, a known friend of Tobias, in charge of the storeroom. We do not know the reasoning behind Nehemiah's decision, but we can guess from experience. In the case of Eliashib's appointment, he violates a cardinal rule for executive leaders: *Never promote your problems.*

I still carry the wounds of making the same mistake. Three or four times in my career, I promoted bright and likeable people into positions of leadership with the assumption that their new role would cover their character flaws. In every case I paid an awful price, and in one case I put my leadership at risk. In yet another, I put a person at a point of where the whole organization could be poisoned. Nehemiah pays the same price. With one bad decision, he opens the door for undoing all the good that he has done in rebuilding the nation upon the moral and spiritual foundation of the Mosaic Law. He may have been naive in his trust of Eliashib, but I doubt it. In the crucible of the cupbearer, he has learned to trust no one. Somehow the scene changes. Perhaps his confidence in the commitment of people who have signed the binding agreement to obey the Law of Moses becomes the basis for his trust. If so, he learns a lesson for all of us. Signed agreements, such as statements of faith or contracts of commitment, are never enough. Nehemiah, a man of total integrity, learns that blind trust is not good enough. Moral agreements must be written into the heart, and spiritual commitments must be etched into the soul. When Nehemiah puts his faith in Eliashib's signature on the binding agreement and assumes that his friendship with Tobias is not contaminating, he puts the moral and spiritual foundation of the nation at risk. Eliashib's corrupt act is contagious. Every moral and spiritual commitment undergirding the nation is violated, and Nehemiah returns home to become a disillusioned leader. It all begins when he overlooks the fatal flaw in Eliashib's character and makes the decision to promote his problem.

Succumbing to Fatigue

How do we account for Nehemiah's lapse in leadership? Experience offers some insights. *At the forefront is the possibility that Nehemiah is showing signs of burnout after 12 years of total self-giving to the rebuilding of the walls and the renewal of the nation.* As a leader who has "been there," I see in Nehemiah the obvious symptoms of emotional exhaustion and executive fatigue. His decision to leave Eliashib in charge of the storehouse in the House of God is a prime example. When leaders are fatigued, mental acuity becomes a blur, and bad decisions are made. Another evidence of burnout is Nehemiah's failure to objectify his role as governor. When the priests, nobles, and officials sin during his absence, he takes their failure personally. Angry and violent actions are justified only if they are not vengeful reactions rising out of personal hurt. When Jesus cleanses the Temple, He shows us objective anger involving principles, not personalities. Nehemiah, on the other hand, pulls the hair out of men who have married foreign wives. In his prayers of remembrance, we can listen between the lines and feel his plea of forgiveness for his own violent acts.

Burnout is an occupational hazard for executive leaders, especially those in top positions. In its extreme form, the symptoms show themselves in such extremes as alcoholism, substance abuse, divorce, mental illness, and even suicide. Other major indicators include physical breakdown, emotional mood swings, and moral confusion. A lesser symptom that hurts executive effectiveness is self-doubt, leading to defensive reactions and bad decisions. In my own case as a chief executive officer, I saw a red light flashing the warning of burnout when I lost the edge of energy, avoided early confrontation to resolve critical issues, magnified minor events into major crises, and became irritable with my wife and family.

The symptoms of burnout are customized for every individual. Wise leaders know their own symptoms and find relief before disaster strikes. Nehemiah's strength of character and spiritual maturity keep him from succumbing to the extreme symptoms of burnout, but he does appear to be a victim of self-doubt and its consequences in defensive reactions and bad decisions.

Futility, however, is the gravest symptom of leadership fatigue. Nehemiah has seen 12 years of sacrifice for his nation and his people wiped out in the brief period of his absence. We can only imagine the agony of starting all over again to reform the nation. In Nehemiah's final prayer, we can hear the plaintive sound of asking, *What is the meaning of my life? Has it been worth it?* His career ends on this sad note of self-pity. With one last plea to be remembered by God, Nehemiah disappears from the scene and leaves no further record of his life or his leadership. A career that begins with a bang ends in a whimper.

Rising to Incompetence

Another option for explaining Nehemiah's apparent failure as a statesman is that he is promoted to the level of his incompe-

tence. Many readers may react negatively to the thought of this option. In all the books that have been written about the leadership of Nehemiah, neither incompetence nor failure is ever mentioned. A working principle of leadership development teaches this to us. None of us has the gifts to lead in every situation, and any one of us can be promoted to our level of incompetence.

In 1980 I came in as runner-up for Secretary of Education in the Reagan cabinet. The nomination was an honor that led to my "15 minutes of fame" in the national media. I am equally quick to admit that I wanted the position and felt as if God's will coincided with my ambition. Still I prayed, *Lord, if being appointed to this position causes me to lose my faith or my family, don't let it happen.* It didn't happen, and thus God answered my prayer. Looking back upon those exhilarating moments at the heights of national visibility, I now realize that God saved me from promotion to the level of my incompetence. I love executive action, but I die in the political process. Others may flourish in the practical art of political compromise, and I honor them. Not me. I have neither the patience nor skills required for the work. If I had been appointed Secretary of Education, I would have rebelled at the appointment of a deputy secretary who was thrust into the position without consulting me, resisted the editing of my speeches for party correctness, and refused to keep my mouth shut in Cabinet meetings when education needed a champion. Indeed, the appointment would have elevated me to my position of incompetence.

Nehemiah may have found himself in the same position. When it comes to managing processes, planning projects, attending to details, and motivating people to perform specific tasks, he is a leader par excellence. These are gifts of leadership that bring him spectacular success in rebuilding the walls of Jerusalem and restoring nationhood to Israel. But when we introduce ambiguity into the plan, add the frustrations of political process, and shift the weight of responsibility from hands-on labor to delegated trust, Nehemiah's experience in the crucible does not transfer. The gifts of an engineer do not apply to the qualifications for a statesman.

Many leaders on the verge of greatness experience the same frustration. Jimmy Carter is a person I have watched throughout his leadership journey from president of the United States to Nobel Peace Prize winner. He brought his engineering skills and his Christian commitment to the presidency and failed, according to the evaluation of most pundits. Rumor has it that he personally reserved the White House tennis courts until the day of his departure. Micromanagement was both his strength and his weakness. Also, when his Christian convictions collided with political advantage, he found himself in a conflict in which he succumbed to political pressure. After losing a second presidential term, however, Jimmy Carter was set free to exercise his gifts. As an engineer giving leadership to the building of homes for the Habitat for Humanity, he feels at home with his gifts. Following the convictions of his Christian faith into the specific tasks of international peace-keeping, he finds his niche. Recently I have been amazed by his venture into the hazardous world of creative fiction with his novel *The Hornet's Nest*. Critics are labeling most of it as "dry as dust," but what else can we expect from a successful engineer? Credit Jimmy Carter with motivation to push the envelop and press himself beyond the limits.

Business Week magazine adds another insight into executive development when it reports on the resignation of Phil

Condit as chairman and chief executive officer of the Boeing Company. In exacting words that cannot be misinterpreted, the article begins with the statement that the story of Phil Condit is

> a tale of a manager promoted beyond his own competence and blind to his own shortcomings. The skills that made him a brilliant engineer—obsessive problem-solving and an ability to envision elegant design solutions—were of less use in the executive position. Although always a bold visionary, Condit was frequently indecisive and isolated as a CEO (*Business Week*, December 15, 2003, 32).

Nehemiah is also a successful engineer who rises to the level of his incompetence. He is a master of a specific task that is narrowly focused upon a detailed plan, implemented by hands-on leadership, and completed in a timely fashion with tangible results. Rebuilding the walls of Jerusalem and the nation of Israel are basically engineering projects at which Nehemiah is highly successful. He also succeeds as governor of the province as long as he is personally present to give hands-on leadership in his role. As soon as he takes a short sabbatical from his post, however, everything falls apart. Israel now needs a leader who is a statesman.

The leadership qualifications for a statesman stand in sharp contrast to the expectations for an engineer. As we have already seen, an engineer works best with a specific task defined by a narrowly focused plan. A statesman does not have that advantage. The task is general, the scope is global, and the plan evolves with the dynamics of demand. An engineer also tends to be a hands-on leader, personally attending to detail and assessing the operation. Again, a statesman can only wish for that advantage. In the give-and-take of political leadership, a statesman must share authority, delegate functions, and depend upon others for effective action. Finally, we remember that an engineer is successful when the process stays on schedule and the results are tangible. Not so for a statesman. Success in leadership is long-term with intangible results. Nehemiah's experience in the crucible of the cupbearer did not prepare him to be a statesman.

Grooming Our Successor

We come to the crux of the problem in the conclusion that *Nehemiah fails to groom a successor who shares his character, vision, and competence.* As we reread Nehemiah's story, we see no evidence of a person to back him up when he has to return to Babylon. Only Eliashib is given leadership responsibility in Nehemiah's absence. Yet his role of minding the central storehouse of the Temple is pivotal to the future of the nation. Because he is Nehemiah's choice for leadership, all other leaders look to him. If he is true to his trust, they will be true to their trust. If he is corrupt, they will be corrupt.

I frequently mentor young college presidents. One of the first questions I ask is, "Assume that you were to drop off the earth tomorrow. Who would continue to carry on your vision and achieve your goals?" Young leaders in particular do not like the question, because they cannot imagine themselves being absent from the scene. Yet it is a lesson that needs to be learned early in an executive career. To identify potential leaders and begin to groom them for a future role is a test of trust and proof of self-confidence. Engineers who depend heavily upon individual expertise have a hard time duplicating themselves. Yet if Nehemiah had been grooming a backup for his leadership, he would have saved himself from the pain of seeing his work unravel.

The harder question is to ask incumbent executives if they are willing to identify and groom young people for the next generation of leadership. An affirmative answer means that they are willing to take on protégés who have the gifts to exceed them. In Nehemiah's case, a successful engineer needs to groom a person with the gifts of a statesman. This is a test of self-sacrifice. Nehemiah would have to see a vision of the future and recognize his own limits. Initially, he might feel a threat from a protégé with the gifts of a statesman, but in the long run he would experience great satisfaction. Rather than closing the Book of Nehemiah with a self-pitying prayer, he could have cast a vision for the future of Israel and commended his successor as the leader of the future.

Developing Our Leadership Exercise 6

Leadership runs in neighborhoods. A neighborhood is more than a single organization or institution. It is a field of service, such as education, business, government, or ministry. We often use the term "Christian community" to describe a large neighborhood in which we serve. Within that neighborhood are sections defined by our theological position or our denominational identity. Most of us spend our careers in one neighborhood or even a section of a neighborhood. Others have the opportunity to change neighborhoods and serve in a wider context.

Think about the neighborhood in which you serve. What is a ministry role to which you might be appointed or elected that would advance you to your level of incompetence? What expectations would either make you uncomfortable or outstrip your competencies?

Extend your thoughts to leadership roles in which you would have to change neighborhoods or bridge across them. What tests of character or competence would come from the new neighborhood? How would these expectations move you to your level of incompetence?

What if you think about these new or expanded responsibilities as a return to the crucible for advanced lessons of leadership? What would you need to learn in order to serve effectively at this level? What would be the tests of character? What would be the tests of competence? Are you ready for such a move? Can you do it? Do you want to do it?

PART 3
IN THE BALANCE

Remember me with favor, O my God (13:31).

—Nehemiah's final word

7
THE PERSPECTIVE OF TIME
THE LONG VIEW OF LEADERSHIP

OUR JOURNEY into leadership is like a quest for the Holy Grail. At the end of our pilgrimage is the hope that we will discover the meaning of greatness. Alas, just like the mythical quest for the Holy Grail, our goal eludes us. We have been fairly successful in identifying some of the characteristics of effective leadership. When the strategic goals of an organization are achieved, leadership is effective. But the same end result cannot be used to differentiate between good and bad leadership. We complicate the issue when a moral standard is added to the equation. Good leaders who are ethical in practice may be ineffective in results. The stage of history is littered with the wreckage of good but ineffective leaders. Bad leaders who violate the standards of right and wrong may actually overachieve their goals. Even if we believe that truth will eventually triumph, we cannot deny the effectiveness of some Machiavellian leaders in reaching their goals.

When we add the idea of "greatness" to the assessment of leadership, we introduce a dimension that is more elusive than ever. Too easily we talk about great leaders, but what do we mean? Nehemiah helps us answer the question. We need an overview of leadership that will balance ethics and effectiveness, goodness and greatness, on an impartial scale.

With that perspective in mind, let's return to the end of Nehemiah's leadership journey.

Back into the Crucible

There are two ways of looking at Nehemiah's final words in his autobiographical book. When he says "Remember me with favor, O God," we can read his words as a sign of resignation or a return to the crucible where there are new things to learn. Pessimists will see his final prayer as a confession of failure; optimists will ask, "What's ahead?"

Crucible experiences are landmarks along the journey of leadership. While one experience may initially shape our character and our competence, every major step forward on the journey will have a crucible of its own. These advanced experiences will test our character and expand our competencies. Through them we realize that leadership is a lifelong learning process. When we stop risking, we stop learning, and when we stop learning, we stop leading. My guess is that any one of us can stop at any given moment and describe the crucible in which we currently find ourselves. It is the heat and pressure of the crucible that divides leaders from nonleaders.

Nehemiah is put back into the crucible by his own mistake. He appoints a man whom he cannot trust into the key position of leadership during his absence. Earlier, after the walls are built, he shows great wisdom in appointing two men to take charge of Jerusalem and assure its security. One leader is his brother, Hanani, who brought Nehemiah the original news about the plight of his people in Jerusalem. Coleadership goes to Hananiah, commander of the citadel, whom Nehemiah commends as "a man of integrity and feared God more than most men do" (7:2). They are given the task of securing the gates of the city by organizing all the residents as "wall-watchers" who back up the official gate-keepers. One can imagine Nehemiah comparing these good appointments with his bad decision to put Eliashib in charge of the central storeroom of the Temple. Good leaders make these comparisons and learn from them. The next time around, Nehemiah will again look for "a man of integrity [who] feared God more than most men do."

What happened to Nehemiah after he finished writing his book? We know that he served as governor of Judah for 12 years (5:14). Then what? Did he leave Jerusalem to resume his position as cupbearer to the king? If so, he must have felt the satisfaction of knowing that he has been faithful to the call of God. At the same time, wouldn't he have missed the challenge of restoring Israel to a place of significance among nations? Perhaps it is my own drive for forward movement that leads me to put the words in Nehemiah's mouth if he was offered his position as cupbearer again: "Been there, done that." His alternative was to breathe another prayer. Everything we know about Nehemiah draws us to the conclusion that he would find meaning in God's will whatever his role would be. We can hear him joining the Bishop of Cambry in his well-known prayer, "Build me up or tear me down—I delight to do thy will, O God."

Failure Is Not Fatal

As our search for greatness in leadership goes on, we encounter a fact that is often blurred by the perspective of time. In every leader's story is a chapter on failure. Howard Gardner's book *Leading Minds* is a psychologist's attempt to get into the minds of 20th-century personalities whom we acclaim as great leaders. Mohandas Gandhi, Eleanor Roose-

velt, Martin Luther King Jr., Margaret Thatcher, J. Robert
Oppenheimer, and Pope John XIII are among his choices.
As diverse as these celebrated figures are, Gardner finds a
common key to understanding their leadership. They share
the ability to create and embody an effective story that they
use to empower ordinary people. But as part of that story,
they all have a chapter on failure. Martin Luther King Jr.,
for example, empowered his people in the rural South, but
could not transfer his story to the urban North or the distant
land of South Africa. Mohandas Gandhi gained his greatness by embodying the ideal of nonviolence but failed to
bring it to reality in his own nation. Pope John XIII is cred-
ited with bringing the Roman Catholic Church into the
20th century, but most of his reforms were not affirmed by
his successors. Do we write these leaders off as failures? Of
course not. When their careers are seen in overview and
with the perspective of time, they are remembered for the
ideals they embodied and the message they communicated
rather than their failures.

Nehemiah deserves his place in biblical history for the
same reason. He, too, shows us the gift of creating, embodying, and communicating a story that empowers ordinary people to achieve great things. It would be wrong to let one bad
decision characterize his life and leadership. Quite to the
contrary, when we see his life and leadership in overview, we
see that he deserves the honor of being known as an engineer
who rebuilds the walls of Jerusalem and a governor who restores the foundations of a nation. His epitaph should not
read, "Remember me with favor, O my God," but rather "I
am carrying on a great project and cannot go down." He is a
builder, and this is his claim to greatness.

Retracing the Journey

To sum up our study of Nehemiah, we need to see his leadership with a bird's-eye view. So far, we have walked with him a step at a time. But when the recorded journey is over, what do we see? The following chart gives us that overview.

Nehemiah's Leadership Development

	Cupbearer	Engineer	Governor
Task:	Protecting the King	Rebuilding the Walls	Renewing the Nation
Scope:	Palace	Jerusalem	Israel
Need:	Survival	Security	Significance
Style:	Authoritarian Control	Transactional Command	Transformational Collaboration
Character:	Loyalty	Consistency	Trust
Competence:	Perfecting Process	Motivating People	Delegating Authority
Resource:	Power	Planning	Persuasion
Conflict:	Conspiracy	Competition	Heresy
Accountability:	King	King/God	King/God/People
Spiritual Life:	Prayers of Preparation	Prayers of Engagement	Prayers of Remembrance
Long-term Goals:	Proof of Process	Completion of Plan	Implementation of Policy

As we review this chart, we realize how far Nehemiah has come in his leadership journey. In the beginning, He might have continued in comfort as the cupbearer to the king, but he could not resist responding to the plight of his people. Taking the ultimate risk, he responds with the integrity of his character and the skills of his leadership. Having walked with him step by step through his journey, we now see his path in overview. For those of us who aspire to higher levels of leadership, Nehemiah shows us what is ahead. As we advance in leadership,

1. Our *task* becomes more complex, ambiguous, and risky.
2. Our *scope* magnifies into a larger scene with greater responsibility.
3. Our *need* rises to moral and spiritual levels.
4. Our *style* becomes more collaborative.
5. Our *competence* shifts toward delegation.
6. Our *resource* leans toward persuasion.
7. Our *conflict* turns inward toward heresy.
8. Our *accountability* is diversified among stakeholders.
9. Our *prayers* are more reflective.
10. Our *goals* tend to be long-term and intangible.

All the glamour of greatness gives way to these realities. Unless a person has the grit as well as the gifts to lead at these advanced levels, greatness will be an elusive dream. Furthermore, we remember that the advancement of godly leadership goes in two directions: upward into visibility and downward into spirituality. No one can survive the lofty spheres of visible leadership without being grounded in the bedrock of spiritual truth. Undergirding Nehemiah's success is his intimate relationship with his God and an unswerving commitment to His Law and His covenant. The Book of Nehemiah is the story of a layman rising high and going down deep.

The Stretch of a Statesman

Nehemiah's challenge to be a statesman is not included on the chart, because it is a logical extension of his leadership as governor. While serving as governor, Nehemiah lays the groundwork for establishing the nation with permanent policies based upon the Law of Moses and the covenant of God. Excelling at this task, he leads Judah into a position of significance among nations. Then, to assure the permanence of these policies for the future of the nation, he is challenged to assume the role of a statesman. With it goes the responsibility for developing leaders who share his vision and embody his message.

The challenge puts Nehemiah back into the fire of the crucible. Known as a hands-on leader who performs miracles in short-term projects, he must now learn new competencies of mentoring, delegating, and trusting. Here is where he struggles, and here is where we learn an invaluable lesson. Every competency has its dark side. Nehemiah excels as an engineer rebuilding the walls, succeeds as a governor rebuilding the nation, but falls short of being a statesman assuring leadership for the future. Few of us can stretch that far. Nehemiah's strength as a hands-on leader becomes his weakness when he must delegate authority to others with full trust and groom the future generation of leaders. We know only that his first decision as a statesman ends in disaster. Because Nehemiah closes his own story with a prayerful sigh of resignation and disappears from further biblical history, we will never know in this life whether he came out of this crucible with the competencies of a statesman or pled to the end of his days, "Remember me with favor, O my God."

So what is greatness in leadership? Does Nehemiah qualify? Our opening question continues to haunt us. Before drawing any conclusion, we need to put Nehemiah's leadership journey into the balance of history.

Developing Our Leadership
Exercise 7

Retrace your own journey using the chart of Nehemiah's leadership development. Ask yourself these questions, and share your answers with a colleague:

1. Which level of leadership—cupbearer, engineer, governor, or statesman—comes closest to describing your present role and responsibility?

2. Which competencies learned in the crucible transfer to your current role, and which do not?

3. If you are rising upward in visibility, are you growing downward in spirituality?

4. What special competencies do you bring to your leadership? What is the dark side of those competencies?

5. As you anticipate the future, what is the leadership role that will take you to your level of incompetence? How will you handle it?

6. Are you identifying potential leaders who share your vision and embody your message? How are you grooming them for future leadership?

Until we ask these questions, we are falling short of our full responsibility as Christian leaders. Jesus is our example. Even though fully God and fully man, He realized the limits of His physical presence and groomed His disciples to fulfill the Great Commission. We can do no less. Leadership for succession is our solemn obligation and joyous opportunity.

I am carrying on a great project and cannot go down (6:3).

—Nehemiah's proof
   of greatness

8
THE SCALE OF GREATNESS
THE QUALITY THAT CANNOT BE TAUGHT

LEADERSHIP THEORY rings with sounds of "effectiveness" and "success." The words are not synonymous. An effective leader is one who achieves stated organizational goals, while a successful leader is one whose accomplishments are lauded by peers or public opinion. Neither term carries moral weight. Hugh Hefner, founder of *Playboy* magazine, is an effective leader in achieving his corporate goals and a successful leader in influencing wholesale attitude change toward sex in the common culture. But if moral values are introduced into the equation, he is a "bad leader" in the view of Bible-believers and a "good leader" in the minds of Generation X. Is there any sense in which he is "great"? If greatness is determined by the accomplishment of goals and the acclaim of success, he is great. If greatness depends upon the leader's embodiment of the message, Hefner's promiscuity is legendary. Or if greatness means cultural transformation of attitudes among the masses, Hefner qualifies for the recognition. If moral and spiritual dimensions are added to the equation, however, Hugh Hefner falls off the scale.

The Quest for Greatness

In his book *Good to Great* Jim Collins identifies five progressive stages of leadership development (20). The first four stages are based upon the competencies of good leadership, beginning with individual skills and rising to teamwork, effective management, and strategic vision and commitment. Stage Five is a jump into greatness. Collins says that a great leader is "humble and fearless." This is the paradoxical quality that sets apart good and great leaders. He goes to add that we can teach leaders the competencies for good leadership, but we cannot teach greatness because we cannot teach humility or fearlessness.

What is the quality of greatness in Christian leadership that cannot be taught? The answer to our question is in the moral and spiritual realm. Seeing once again the overview of Nehemiah's leadership journey, we realize that there is a "constant" that does not change as he moves forward into new challenges. His personal integrity is never compromised, and his spiritual relationship with God is never broken. These are qualities that cannot be taught. They must be experienced by faith and fulfilled by grace. Humility, then, is a natural by-product, because godly leaders depend upon resources that are not their own. Based upon these criteria, Nehemiah qualifies for greatness even though he never makes the roll call of the heroes of faith in the Book of Hebrews or finishes his career in a blaze of glory.

We cannot stop here. A journey into greatness includes "willfulness" as another quality that is recognized in both secular and Christian theory. Warren Bennis calls this quality "persistence" in his book *Leaders: Four Strategies for Taking Charge* (45). One of the four strategies that the authors recommend is "trust through positioning." They are referring to a leader to takes a position and holds it with persistence. The authors are endorsing consistency, not rigidity. Trust, the highest hope of leadership, is the result. Nehemiah shows us this strategy during the rebuilding of the walls as well as in the rebuilding of the nation. Despite all the obstacles that confront him, he does not waver in his position. When Sanballat woos him to leave his work and come down from the walls for a summit meeting to iron out their differences, Nehemiah demonstrates the meaning of "trust through positioning" for all future leaders. We can only imagine the response of his fellow laborers when they hear him say, "I am carrying on a great project and cannot go down." Hope rises and doubts disappear as the people go back to their work with renewed vigor.

In one of my books on leadership, I make the statement "Faithfulness, not success, is the standard for Christian leadership" (David L. McKenna, *Never Blink in a Hailstorm and Other Lessons on Leadership* [Grand Rapids: Baker Books, 2005], 24). A marketer who reviewed the manuscript wrote back to say that this approach would never sell. Young leaders, he said, are interested only in promotion and success. Perhaps he is right. If so, it illustrates how wide the disjuncture is between secular and Christian leadership. Success is not a biblical concept. Whenever it rears its ugly head in the presence of Jesus, He rejects it. The parable of the talents is just one of many illustrations. When the stewards return with a report on the investment of their talents, the master honors those who have multiplied their original gift with the commendation "Well done, good and faithful servant! You have been faithful with a few things; I will put you in charge of many things" (Matt. 25:23). Jesus is enunciating a biblical principle for us. Faithfulness partners with goodness as the standard for greatness in Christian servanthood.

I learned this lesson while writing the *Communicator's Commentary on Isaiah.* In the overquoted and underpreached account of Isaiah's confrontation with the holy God in chapter 6, most preachers stop with the prophet's response, "Here am I. Send me!" (Isa. 6:8). They miss the rest of the story. Isaiah now hears the details of his calling from God: "Go and tell this people . . ."—a message they will hear but not understand, see but not perceive. If they do, they will have to turn from their wicked ways in order to be healed (Isa. 6:9-10). Isaiah protests, "For how long, O Lord?" (Isa. 6:11). God's answer is not easy for those of us who are the children of a ready answer and a quick fix. He tells His chosen prophet that he is to remain faithful to his message even though the people will not hear and even though he will be long gone before his prophetic word comes true and the promise of the Messiah is fulfilled (Isa. 6:11-13).

Radical Faithfulness

Faithfulness takes on radical new dimensions in God's response to Isaiah's plea. It is more than achieving instant results and greater than winning the acclaim of public success. A leader who is faithful despite public rejection or faithful to a vision that will not be realized in his or her lifetime is the true candidate for greatness.

It is time to draw a line, not just in the sand but in the annals for defining greatness in leadership. The success syndrome in leadership development needs to be exposed as counter-Christian, along with the prosperity gospel for preaching, the entertainment motive for worship, and the market mentality for church growth. Faithfulness must take its place as a quality of leadership that cannot be taught. Furthermore, we dare not shy away from the radical nature of faithfulness in biblical terms. Godly leaders are called to be faithful to God's *task* without the assurance of success, faithful to God's *message* without the assurance of being heard, and faithful to God's *vision* without the assurance of seeing it realized.

How does Nehemiah measure up to this standard for greatness? His willingness to go to Jerusalem to rebuild the walls against overwhelming odds is witness to his faithfulness to his task without the assurance of success. His persistence in renewing and reforming the nation testifies to his faithfulness to his message without the assurance of being heard. His disappearance from the stage of history after his final efforts at reform confirms his faithfulness to a vision without the assurance of seeing it realized.

Let there be no mistake: faithfulness is not a substitute for ineffectiveness or an excuse for the lack of results. The lack of competence is no more acceptable in the development of Christian leadership than the lack of character. Nehemiah is a competent leader with the evidence of results and the record of success. Even after making the mistake of appointing Eliashib to guard the central storehouse of the Temple, he wastes no time in confronting the culprits and cleaning up the corruption. Character and competence march hand in hand through his leadership journey.

A Nagging Question

What happens to Nehemiah after he finishes his term as governor and returns to the court of King Artaxerxes? I must confess that I cringe at the thought of Nehemiah returning to his former role as cupbearer after he finishes his term as governor. Because I have been thoroughly immersed in the success syndrome based upon progress and promotion, I cannot conceive a U-turn on our leadership journey that takes us back to an earlier and lesser role. So often I have testified that God always leads us forward into ever wider and brighter horizons in His goodwill. I have also claimed that as pioneers of faith, we never circle the wagons for self-protection. So when opportunities come to speak in conferences, attend events of honor, or serve on boards and committees that are repeats from the past, behind my RSVP declining the invitation is the muttered comment, "Been there, done that."

Retirement is putting a different spin on the idea of moving onward and upward on an unending journey. Suddenly I find myself without leadership position, title, or task. In one sense, it might mean that the leadership journey has come to an end. With each year of age, the invitations for active engagement in speaking, consulting, and serving on boards or committees continue to shrink in number. I confess that I still need to be wanted and esteemed, but the Spirit of God is teaching me otherwise. After years of executive action in an academic setting, His Spirit has set me on a path going forward in the greater realms of mind and spirit. I no longer have to read books just to keep up with my field, and I no longer have to pray just for strength to keep up with administrative demands. More and more, I find myself returning to the classics in order to backfill a hole in my liberal education, enlarging my sphere of prayer to neighborhood children for whom I am "Grandpa Dave," and learning what it means to weep with those who are grieving, hurt, and helpless.

Leading from the Bottom Up

Throughout the writing of this book, I felt the frustration of not knowing what happened to Nehemiah after he closed the book that bears his name. A wakeful moment in the middle of the night brought an insight prompted by the Spirit of God. I realized that I had been looking at Nehemiah's leadership journey from the top down rather than the bottom up. I was a victim of the mentality that speaks of servant-leadership but practices leader-servanthood. Let's face it. Even in the Christian community, we exalt leadership and tolerate servanthood. Jesus turns this kind of thinking on its ear when He says, "If anyone wants to be first, he must be the very last, and the servant of all" (Mark 9:35). He leaves no doubt about the order of servanthood and leadership. Yet as we think about our obsession with the subject of leadership, we must confess that the order is switched. Greatness is defined by leadership, and goodness is defined by servanthood. Within this framework, Nehemiah becomes a leader who is good but not great—unless we think otherwise.

When I introduced Nehemiah at the beginning of his journey into leadership, I wrote, "Each time I read Nehemiah's story, I am stopped by his statement 'I was a cupbearer for the king.'" Now, as we arrive at the end of his journey, the words come back again like a flash of light to awaken our understanding. Nehemiah is a servant bearing the king's cup from beginning to end. Even though he is vaulted into a 12-year stint as a leader in Judah, he still sees his primary role as servant to the king. This answers the question about Nehemiah's future after he rebuilds the walls of Jerusalem and renews the nation of Israel. He returns to his permanent role as cupbearer and continues to serve until he retires or dies. As Paul Harvey would say, "Now you know the rest of the story!"

An Unwritten Postscript

Nehemiah is the hero of common people. He sees himself as a servant rather than a leader. He exercises simple faith rather than seeing a grandiose vision. He functions in a routine role rather than a glamorous job. He is member of the laity rather than the priesthood. He is an engineer rather than an entrepreneur. He volunteers to serve a human need rather than answering the call to lead a nation. He asks for grace rather than power. He asks others to help rather than doing it all himself. He serves selflessly rather than exploiting his perks. He identifies with the poor rather than the powerful. He maintains his integrity rather than succumbing to flattery. He excels in a tangible task rather than trying to win the world. He accepts the limits of his leadership rather than overplaying his hand. He makes a timely exit rather than overstaying his time. He returns to his servant role rather than hanging on to the vestiges of leadership. If asked the question, "Do you see yourself as a servant or a leader?" we can be sure that Nehemiah would simply say, "I was cupbearer to the king." In his answer, we understand why biblical scholars see Nehemiah as a Christ model. He incarnates the Spirit of God in everyday existence, serves human need out of love for God, obeys the will of God to the very end, and leaves the scene counting upon God to honor his faithfulness. At the very least, Nehemiah and Jesus are soul brothers.

Is Nehemiah a great leader? No—if we assume that great leaders rise to heights of visible stature and go out in a blaze of glory. Yes—if we take seriously the words of Jesus when He says, "Whoever wants to be great among you must be your servant, and whoever wants to be first must be slave of all" (Mark 10:43-44). And yes again—if we believe that faithfulness and humility are qualities of servanthood that cannot be taught.

Nehemiah's story has a final word for the development of godly leaders in our generation. In the leadership journey from goodness to greatness, our constant prayer must be that those who come after us will find that we were faithful to our God.

Or if we were to etch Nehemiah's epitaph in stone for all future generations to read, what greater tribute could be given than to remember a humble servant by his own words: "I was cupbearer to the king."

Developing Our Leadership
Exercise 8

If Christian leadership begins with self-death, and if greatness begins with servanthood, most of the current theories about leadership development are turned upside down. As a Christian leader, whether clergy or laity, ask yourself the following questions with brutal honesty.

- Is my primary motivation to be a servant or a leader?
- How would my superiors, peers, and subordinates answer the same question about me?

If you identify yourself as a "servant-leader," how do you reconcile the competing expectations of being a "servant" and a "leader"?

Think of a great Christian leader whom you know. How do humility and faithfulness distinguish his or her greatness?

If humility and faithfulness cannot be taught, how can they be learned? Is the crucible test of character and competence also the classroom for greatness?

How is the Holy Spirit teaching you to be humble and faithful?

If you were to write your own epitaph, how would you want it read?

A final word of encouragement for current and developing Christian leaders: greatness in Christian leadership is like joy in Christian living. If you pursue it, it eludes you; but once your focus is on the Holy One, you will be surprised. Jesus whets our appetite for the element of surprise when He foresees the final procession into the Kingdom of heaven when "many who are first will be last, and the last first" (Mark 10:31). Think of the privilege of marching through the gates arm in arm with Nehemiah!